SCHLEIERMACHER'S SOLILOQUIES

SCHLEIERMACHER'S SOLILOQUIES

AN ENGLISH TRANSLATION
OF
THE MONOLOGEN

WITH A CRITICAL INTRODUCTION
AND APPENDIX

BY

HORACE LELAND FRIESS

ASSISTANT PROFESSOR OF PHILOSOPHY
IN COLUMBIA UNIVERSITY

Wipf and Stock Publishers
150 West Broadway • Eugene OR 97401

Wipf and Stock Publishers
150 West Broadway
Eugene, Oregon 97401

Schleiermacher's Soliloquies
An English Translation of the Monologen with a Critical Introduction and Appendix
By Friess, Horace Leland
ISBN: 1-57910-855-5
Publication date: January, 2002
Previously published by Open Court Publishing Company, 1926.

TO
FELIX ADLER

IN GRATEFUL AND AFFECTIONATE
APPRECIATION

PREFACE

SCHLEIERMACHER'S *Soliloquies* (*Monologen*) were written a few months after the *Speeches on Religion*, his best known work, and the two supplement each other. In Germany the *Soliloquies* have been, like Fichte's *Vocation of Man* which bears the same date, one of the few original expressions of philosophic idealism to become a popular classic. The text appeared in four editions during Schleiermacher's life, in 1800, 1810, 1822, and 1829. Thereafter it was republished in 1836, in 1843, 1846, 1848, 1853, 1860, in 1866 by two different publishers, again in 1869, and in 1870. Since then it has been incorporated as a German classic in various libraries such as *Reclams Universalbibliothek* and *Hendels Bibliothek der Gesamtliteratur* also in *Meyers Volksbücher*. In 1902 Friedrich Michael Schiele of Marburg University published a critical edition, which has been several times reprinted, and is by far the most useful edition for scholars. This is the edition used in making the present translation. A French translation was printed in 1837 and republished in 1864, but until now no English translation has appeared.

In making his critical edition Schiele used the original version of 1800 for the main body of his text, and I have followed him in this respect. In footnotes he put the numerous changes made by Schleiermacher in the second and third editions, 1810 and 1822 respectively. The greater number of these changes are purely stylistic, but there are some important revisions of the thought also. I have not translated those footnotes of Schiele's which contain the purely stylistic changes, since these can be of interest only to a reader of German, but I have included in notes of my own all the material changes. (See pp. 104-112.)

Most of the English literature on Schleiermacher has been concerned primarily with his work as a theologian. The philosophical current underlying this work has scarcely been tapped. In my Introduction I have tried to characterize the romantic spirituality of the *Soliloquies*, to show its origins in the growth of our culture and its relations to modern religious currents. This theme seems to me to be the most significant one in the first half of Schleiermacher's life, that is from 1768-1800.

The second half of his life, from 1800-1834, is another story, and one that I have not attempted to tell on the same scale, partly because it is so different a story as to require another book, and still more because the materials for it have not yet been adequately sifted by those who know the sources to make its general significance accessible. The materials themselves, i. e., the systematic philosophical works of Schleiermacher's later years, in the present state of their editing and interpretation are of interest to the special student only. For the use of such special students, who can not read German, I have added an appendix, giving a brief account of the dialectical development of Schleiermacher's philosophy, especially in his later years. (See pp. 113ff.)

Professor John J. Coss of Columbia University, who first suggested to me that a translation of the *Monologen* would be desirable, has faithfully sponsored the project with constructive suggestions throughout. In the course of my work I have also come into closer touch with the thought of three teachers, John Dewey, F. J. E. Woodbridge, and Felix Adler, to whom I am indebted for fundamental ideas of great value, not only for my immediate purpose, but far beyond it. Dr. Adler has taken an especially helpful interest in the translation. My friends, James Gutmann and J. H. Randall, Jr., have given no end of encouragement and help to the last detail. Finally, I wish to acknowledge some special points of advice and criticism given by Professor J. Bauer of Heidelberg and Dr. A. C. McGiffert of Union Theological Seminary. To each and all of these I extend warm thanks.

HORACE L. FRIESS.

COLUMBIA UNIVERSITY, May, 1926.

TABLE OF CONTENTS

Introduction	xi
Schleiermacher's Soliloquies	1
Reflection	10
Soundings	26
The World	49
Prospect	69
Youth and Age	89
Schleiermacher's revisions of the text	104
Appendix	115
I. The development of Schleiermacher's philosophical system	115
II. Schleiermacher's conception of a philosopher-priest	149
Selected Bibliography	167
Index	171

INTRODUCTION

THE impulse to make open confession, to reveal the counsels of the heart, or to write spiritual autobiography seems particularly strong in religious souls, and has in all times and places left an intimate record of religious experience. Schleiermacher's *Soliloquies* (*Monologen*) is a record of this type, although it contains nothing, as its author says, of religion in a strict and narrow sense.[1] It is an inner conversation, a series of meditations, a book of self-scrutiny. It is one of the very few writings in the literature of German philosophic idealism, which imparts experiences and beliefs directly instead of through a medium of speculation and dialectic. It supplements the argued apology for religion, with which Schleiermacher's name is pre-eminently associated, by a more immediate revelation of his own distinctive spirituality. There is no more immediate and representative a revelation than the *Soliloquies* of that peculiar speculative and romantic idealism which has so thoroughly permeated German thought from 1800 to the very present. The chief fruits of Schleiermacher's life are no doubt to be found in his works on religion, especially in his noted book *On Religion: Speeches addressed to its cultured despisers* (1799), but what his life was in its spiritual essence, when he

[1] See below pp. 6.

wrote this evangel of modernist Protestantism—and thereby much of the meaning of what he said—is more purely revealed in the *Soliloquies* of a year later.[2]

The history of Schleiermacher's family is linked with three distinct episodes in the development of liberal Protestantism, each of which has produced a characteristic strain of thought and feeling in pursuit of a characteristic kind of liberation.[3] The first strain is that common initially to the Quakers and Pietists, then to Wesleyanism, and evangelicalism generally. It is essentially bent on inner moral regeneration, often strongly tinged with elements of mystical exaltation. It is supernaturalistic at first hand or by original conviction. Its liberalism consists in its freedom from ecclesiastical forms, and its reliance upon the individual's experience. It was evoked essentially by the ecclesiastical formalism of the seventeenth century, by sectarian strife and those last fearful struggles over the dead body of mediaeval Christendom, that raged in Central Europe from 1618 to 1648. Above the degradation and turmoil of those years there came once more to certain sensitive souls a pure vision of Christ, still beckoning to all men as a companion in a simple but adequate brotherhood of charity. For these idealists the immediate communion with Christ was the supreme reality of life. One might walk and talk with Him in the fields around Bristol or in the

[2] Cf. p. 99 below and note *. When citing the German text of the *Monologen* I shall refer to the critical edition by F. M. Schiele and designate it *Schiele*. See Bibliography, p. 167.

[3] In Catholic Christianity, in Judaism, in all western religion there have been analogous movements, but I shall confine myself to Protestantism within which Schleiermacher's influence has been immediate and decisive.

Rhineland, as every Pietist and Methodist hymn-book testifies.

The same century that produced the founders of evangelicalism witnessed the impressive discovery of the Newtonian system of nature. As the fact of natural law gradually permeated the minds of people, a new and very different type of liberal Protestantism developed. Its aim was to free the religious tradition of elements which might impede the development of natural knowledge. It sought to eliminate extravagant supernaturalism, and to grasp "the analogy of religion to the constitution and order of nature." Its liberalism was that of freedom from superstition, of encouraging solid thought in the furtherance of human welfare.

For a time this humanitarian program of eighteenth century rationalism seemed to advance along simple lines. But gradually with the accumulation of knowledge and power, the constitution and order of nature were seen to be more complicated than hitherto supposed, and the elements of human welfare to be more varied. The nineteenth century produced a bewildering variety both of theoretical and of practical perspectives. It would be hard to say where the choice of reason is most difficult: whether in the field of metaphysics, beset as it is, on the side of natural philosophy, with the problems of interpreting evolution and relativity (not to mention the claim of metaphysical idealism to supplant all naturalism), or in the field of competing economic interests, or yet again in the realm of contrary cultural ideals. This new situation has given rise to another form of religious liberalism, namely modernism. The liberalism of the modernist is that of the romanticist, who feels the appeal of multifarious attractions. It is no longer the eighteenth century problem of assimilating natural law alone that besets the modernist, but rather that of absorbing a great variety of new goods and powers, of keeping abreast with the times in their giddy course. Hence the term "modernist" is appropriate. His problem is essentially to find what place and meaning his religion may claim to have amid all this welter of modern interests.

Schleiermacher's thought is an early episode in the emergence of modernism, but the history of his forbears reflects the still earlier phases of liberal Protestantism.[4] His paternal grandfather had been a religious radical of the evangelistic type, while his father, also a churchman, inclined toward rationalism. The grandfather, Daniel Schleiermacher, had been a leading supporter of Eller, whose mystical, apocalyptic gospel, typical of the emotional piety prevalent in his day, caused considerable stir in the Rhineland during the 1730's and 40's. When the Ellerian sect fell into discredit, due to the misconduct of its founder, Daniel Schleiermacher suffered not only loss of prestige, but was accused of practicing sorcery and of lèse-majesté. An order was issued for his arrest, but he escaped capture by flight to Arnheim. This was in 1749, scarcely twenty years before the birth of his illustrious grandson, Friedrich. The experience of these difficulties seems to have produced in his son, Gottlieb, a restrained critical temper and especially a suspicion of

[4] For the family history, see pp. 3-11; N. E. 3-12 of Wilhelm Dilthey's *Leben Schleiermachers*. This standard biography will be referred to hereafter as *Dilthey*. The initials N. E. precede page references to the New Edition by Herm. Mulert, 1922.

enthusiasm in matters of religion. He clung to the orthodox church, as indispensable for the moral education of the lower classes. Indeed, he became an army chaplain, but he confesses to have preached "for twelve years virtually without belief."[5] This attitude of accommodation to the institution of the church was as typical in his generation as Eller's mysticism had been in the previous one, but Gottlieb Schleiermacher does not seem to have been happy in it. He wanted his children to grow up in a warmer and deeper Christian feeling, and as he and his wife had been impressed on their travels with the piety of the Moravian communities, he decided to send his son Friedrich and his daughter Charlotte to school in one of these communities at Niesky in Upper Lusatia.

Friedrich Schleiermacher was fourteen years old when he came to Niesky in 1783 and he stayed with the Moravians for four years. Thus he spent these very impressionable years of his life in an atmosphere of evangelical piety, but the result was not a return to the religion of his grandfather (nor a persistence in the rationalism of his father), but rather the emergence of a third type of liberal Protestantism, which was to become characteristic of the nineteenth century. In some respects evangelical piety took hold of him deeply. For instance, he seems very soon to have experienced a full-fledged conviction of sin. At least he took his own deficiencies very seriously, and wrote after a short time in the brotherhood: "I have experi-

[5] See Schleiermacher's *Letters*, v. 1, p. 84. Hereafter I shall refer to these volumes simply as *Letters*, or as *Briefe* in the case of those volumes which have not been translated into English. Volume I contains a short autobiographical sketch up to the year 1794.

ençed much, that is, much of evil on my part and much of grace on the part of heaven. On my part, I have deserved wrath! But the Lamb of the Cross cries to me: 'I have atoned for thee!' "[6] The experience of grace, however, did not develop as it should. And Schleiermacher had in its place imaginative moments, in which he wondered whether all the legend of Christianity, as well as all the stories he had been told of ancient history, were not purely fanciful.

These random doubts of childhood were in time suppressed, but only by the satisfaction of a growing critical faculty—not by acquiescence in tradition, but by the getting of new knowledge. There was a fellow-student in the school at Niesky named Albertini, and a teacher, named Hilmer, who aroused in Schleiermacher a greater passion for learning, in particular for classical literature, than the place could satisfy. The Moravian system showed a shrewd appreciation of worldly commonsense, but the uncommon achievements of worldly-minded genius, like natural science and classical literature, it generally neglected. Its deepest vein was other-worldly, and it found greater value in spontaneous inner lights, in dreams and unexpected revelations of the supernatural, than in learning. At the Moravian seminary in Barby, to which he was promoted after two years, Schleiermacher felt the limitations of Moravianism more sharply than at the school. No attention was paid to the renaissance in letters, in scholarship, and in philosophy that was even then raising the German mind to its highest spiritual achievements. There was an index of forbidden

[6] *Letters*, v. 1, pp. 1-45, quotation from p. 38. See also *Dilthey*, pp. 12-21; N. E. 13-28 for these school-days.

literature, both ancient and modern. Schleiermacher found some congenial fellow-spirits among the students with whom he formed his first real friendships, and together they smuggled some of the condemned books into the school, among them Wieland's poems and Goethe's *Werther.* Their friendship, formed under the golden spell of Greek naturalism and modern poetry, took on an ideal significance. They regarded themselves as harbingers of a better era for humanity, working in secret.[7] But relations with the authorities of the seminary became more and more unbearable.

The great University of Halle, only a few miles away, was under these circumstances an irresistible temptation. In 1787, after two years in the seminary, Schleiermacher made the final decision to break away from the Moravian Brotherhood, and wrote to his father for permission to study at Halle. His father was deeply grieved, and for a time irate, but finally he gave his full consent. In these letters to his father Schleiermacher put certain theological doubts in the foreground as reasons for his break with the Moravians, questioning especially their naively supernatural Christology.[8] This was an issue which his father and his father's generation, given to rationalism and deism, would understand and would regard as crucial. But for Schleiermacher himself it was only half the story. A new world of esthetic feeling, of historic research, of social relations was opening to his imagination and to that of his young companions, a world unknown to the eighteenth century. Toward this world of the

[7] Cf. the later expression of this feeling among the romanticists. See below pp. 61ff.
[8] *Letters,* v. 1, pp. 46-67ff. contains this significant series of letters between Schleiermacher and his father.

future Schleiermacher went when he left the Moravians.

But he took with him a permanent heritage of his early training. The four years spent in the Moravian Brotherhood not only associated his life and his ideals inseparably with Christian religion, but also determined in great measure the form that Christianity, and religion as a whole, thereafter took in his mind. Among the Moravians he had experienced conversion, redemption, regeneration, and other-worldliness as emotional facts, and these experiences remained a part of himself, though he left the cult and its theology. ("Religion remained with me," he wrote later, "when God and immortality vanished before my doubting eyes."[9]) The deep humility of the Moravians, their utter trust in Providence, left in him a permanent quality of reverence, a basic tranquility and repose, and holiness of spirit.[10] He was likewise imbued with the personalism, the moral earnestness of brother in dealing with brother. These positive qualities of Moravian piety were firmly grounded in Schleiermacher, and remained in him as a permanent spiritual deposit conditioning his whole subsequent growth.

When he went to Halle, he enrolled as a theological student, thus continuing, despite his break with the Moravians, in the clerical traditions of his family. He

[9] *Über die Religion: Reden an die Gebildeten unter ihren Verächtern* (1st ed., republished by R. Otto, Göttingen, 1920), p. 10. Hereafter I cite this edition as *Reden*, and the English translation by John Oman, London, 1894, as *On Religion*. This English translation is of Schleiermacher's revised text, and contains interesting variations. For example, the passage quoted above reads: "When the God and immortality of my childhood vanished from my doubting eyes, piety remained to me." See p. 9, also pp. 275-284, of Oman's translation.

[10] Cf. below p. 154.

says he could imagine no means but preaching for exerting the particular didactic influence upon the spirit of the common man, that seemed a part of his nature.[11] And so he clung to the plan of preaching throughout many years of groping. All through his university days, however, and for years afterward, even though he had begun to preach, he could find little joy in "theological rubbish."[12] His favorite studies were those in ancient literature and in philosophy. At Halle he was fortunate to have teachers of an ability commensurate with his ambition in these subjects, F. A. Wolf, one of the founders of modern classical scholarship, and E. A. Eberhard, who emphasized the continuity of modern philosophical thought with the Greek tradition and criticized the Kantian revolution. Eberhard set Schleiermacher to work translating Aristotle's *Ethics*.[13] The discipline of original research under the guidance of these men gave him a critical sense for fact and a training in exact, systematic thought.

The scientific tradition to which Schleiermacher was introduced at Halle was predominantly rationalistic. Science was conceived as a development of propositions tested by their relations to each other. Experience was taken into account by the recognition that the material for the formulation of propositions is furnished by experience and by the expectation that falsifications of experience will reveal themselves in the form of conflicting propositions. In this form of rationalism the antithesis between logic and experi-

[11] *Letters*, v. 1, p. 177.
[12] *Briefe*, v. 4, p. 42.
[13] Cf. below p. 117, note 5. Cf. *Dilthey*, pp. 28-36; N. E. 39-47.

ence, which has furnished such a dilemma for the theory of knowledge, is somewhat mitigated. The network of propositions that constitute science is regarded as a network in which experience (and thereby the stuff of the world) is caught up. Schleiermacher was brought up in this view of science as an ordered whole, and he never abandoned it, even though he became clearly conscious of difficulties involved in it. He saw that, according to this view, the certainty of specific propositions depends on their relations to the whole body of truth; the fact that we do not know this whole tends to infect all our knowledge with uncertainty and to make our rationalistic systems somewhat inadequate and artificial. We are forced to be experimental, sceptical, and intuitive, in the interest of the fullness of life and being that lies beyond our organized thought. Instead of taking these freer activities into his conception of science, however, Schleiermacher prefers to think of them as belonging to the highly important, non-scientific side of life. The ideal of science itself is to be purely rational, and in his formal, scientific works of later years he shows an arduous loyalty to this ideal by casting all his demonstrations into a rigid, systematic form.[14] The rationalistic ideal of science is maintained as expressing an unattainable perfection of one of man's eternal interests. But since it is clearly recognized to be both an unattainable and a one-sided interest, there appears in Schleiermacher's philosophy a certain antithesis or

[14] Cf. below pp. 132ff. in connection with above discussion, and also the collected edition of Schleiermacher's works, part III, vol. 5, pp. 3-8, 24-25, and part III, vol. 4², pp. 144ff. Hereafter I shall refer to this edition as *Werke,* and use numerals I, II, and III to designate the theological, homiletic, and philosophical divisions respectively. See Bibliography, p. 167 below.

tension, very characteristic and fundamental in all German thought of recent times, between the supposed claims of order and system, on the one hand and the supposed claims of life and being, on the other. Certain underlying motives and causes of this very characteristic antithesis will appear in further tracing Schleiermacher's development.

The interest of his teachers at Halle and of their better pupils in Greek thought marks a turning point in the development of modern philosophy. After a period of comparative neglect, a revival of classical studies made its appearance in the eighteenth century, which brought Schleiermacher and many of his contemporaries under its spell. In the same years that he was translating Aristotle at Halle, Friedrich Schlegel was studying Greek poetry at Leipzig and Dresden, Schelling Greek mythology at Tübingen, and Hegel Greek religion in Tübingen and Basel. (That these early studies of the German philosophers were not merely school-boy exercises will scarcely be questioned, yet it is interesting to quote from a letter of Hegel's which shows plainly what was really at stake in them. Congratulating J. C. Voss on his translation of Homer's *Odyssey*, Hegel writes: "Luther translated the Bible, and you have translated Homer into German; it is my work *to translate philosophy into our tongue.*"[15]) This approach to philosophy through its history, which was the approach of Schleiermacher as well as of Hegel, differentiates the spirit of these men sharply from that of their seventeenth and eighteenth century predecessors. The great pioneers of modern philosophy had

[15] G. W. F. Hegel, *Werke*, v. xix, p. 52. See also Schleiermacher's *Letters*, v. 1, p. 14.

largely believed with Descartes that literary and historical studies were a temptation to be avoided in favor of the more serious pursuit of mathematics. Such intellectual puritanism had its moral counterpart in the prudence with which the middle classes, amid the wantonness of arbitrary government and religious fanaticism, laid the economic foundations of their well-being. An appreciation of rational order was for them, as for the philosophers, the highest wisdom, and for a brief time in the eighteenth century religious feeling fastened on cogency and order as the supreme evidence of divinity. But the same century also witnessed a change of temper at the close. Coincident with increased prosperity and the recognized triumph of modern society over mediaevalism and feudalism, came the awakening of new desires and a general widening of interests. Security and order, once established, were no longer the ideal; variety and fullness of life took their place. People discovered the bareness of puritan rationalism, and demanded a richer measure of thought and feeling. The revival of interest in ancient Greek culture was but one item in a romantic program of general spiritual expansion.

It is customary to contrast this new romantic temper of mind with the rationalism that preceded it, to set the philosophy of spirit which it produced over against the seventeenth and eighteenth century philosophy of nature. But underlying both the ideal of rational order and the romantic ideal, as a continuous historical process, was the making of modern society with a new system of natural and civil law. The French Revolution was neither the beginning nor the end of this process, but simply inaugurated a phase of freer expansion, and it was this opportunity of freer expansion that excited the romantic temper of mind. When the ideal of civil liberty was once established as a political force, the emancipation movement, far from disappearing, became universal and polymorphous. Similarly, the idea of scientific inquiry did not disappear in romanticism, but was extended from the field of nature to other fields, and surrounded with new emotional values. Science came to be conceived as a function of Spirit, a phase in the life of reason, not merely as an inquiry into the laws of nature. It sometimes seems as if romanticism had carried us far from a rational pursuit of liberty and truth. It has made the pursuit more difficult, because it has manifolded and enriched the meaning of liberty and truth. But this very quality of manifold and enriched idealism, with all its characteristic antitheses, which is the essence of romanticism, implies a continuity with modern society in its simpler beginnings, such as would permit the gradual accumulation of many purposes. Had there been a real break with the past and a new beginning in the nineteenth century (e. g., like that involved in the rise of new peoples within the Roman Empire), the new spirit of that century could scarcely have been modern romanticism.

The gradual transition to romanticism seemed all the more like an absolute break with the past and a radically new beginning, because it coincided with a shift in philosophic leadership from Great Britain and France to Germany. The fact that romantic idealism received its most impressive philosophic statement in Germany rather than in another country, and hence that it was permeated with German characteristics, has tended to an identification or at least to the assumption of an essential connection between the German spirit and the romantic spirit. But it was the circumstances under which German philosophy was made, fully as much as the influence of German character, that caused the greatest creation of Germany in the realm of philosophy to be a romantic type of metaphysics. It was not the romantic character of all things German that caused romanticism to find its classic expression in Weimar, Jena, and Berlin. (The ingredients or elements of a work like *Faust* are many of them quite the opposite of romantic; it is their combination, the attempt to embrace magic and science, poetry and politics, Hellenism and Protestantism, romance and toil in the compass of a single life that is strikingly romantic and peculiar to the ambitions of modern society become conscious of its diverse riches.) It was rather the fact that all things German were being gathered up into classic syntheses at a time when the prevailing mentality was romantic. And this fact in turn can not be attributed solely to the influence of great individuals, who happened to be Germans, like Immanuel Kant and Goethe. A combination of many historic circumstances brought the making of German cultural traditions in a special measure under the influence of romanticism, and hence reciprocally the romantic movement enjoyed a larger measure of life in Germany than anywhere else, and received a strong German coloring. Germany as such was just beginning to exist, the various forces of her life were fruitfully combining with each other, when modern society reached that stage of development which provoked the romantic temper, and hence in Germany the romantic movement coincided with a great national awakening. To glorify manifold activity and differentiation at the beginning of the nineteenth century meant in Germany to participate actually in the integration and molding of a new national life. It was the force of this opportunity that made German poets and philosophers in fullest measure the interpreters of this particular moment in western civilization.

While German philosophy was still predominantly rationalistic in spirit, still under the sway of Leibniz and Wolff, eighteenth century British and French thought had gone a long way toward transforming and undermining the intellectual orthodoxy of enlightened rationalism. The emergence of romantic concepts and categories came gradually, in different ways for different minds, but the final, decisive influence for Schleiermacher and for most of his German contemporaries at least were the ideas of Immanuel Kant. While Schleiermacher was still a student at the University of Halle, the first wave of Kantianism swept over Germany, and poured through the crumbling walls of orthodox rationalism. His teacher, Eberhard, was not much impressed with this new "critical philosophy,' but Schleiermacher was prepared to study his Kant alone. After leaving the University in 1789, he went to live with his uncle, a professor of theology well-acquainted with Sack, the court-preacher to Frederick the Great and with other élite of the Reformed Church in Germany. The library and companionship of his uncle were intended to help him prepare for the theological examinations required of all candidates for the ministry, but Schleiermacher apparently gave more attention to Kant than to theology. In 1790 he wrote to a friend "my belief in the Kantian philosophy increases daily, especially as I compare it with the Leibnizean."[16]

For Leibniz the major aspects of the world were determined by the great structures of mathematical physics, Christian theology, and civil law; the business of philosophy was to understand the nature of these structures so as to assure their harmonious development. Among such definitely ordered materials rationalism was very much at home, and felt confident to sketch out a plan of the entire universe. Schleiermacher was separated from this point of view, not by his own individual thinking, but by a whole century of change which many minds had jointly produced, and which affected all his contemporaries. Through the gradual accumulation of new knowledge and new powers, the sharpening of criticism and the awakening of new interests, the structures underlying the metaphysics of rationalism were being rapidly outgrown. In England John Locke developed an empirical psychology which showed, as Berkeley pointed out, the irrelevance of mathematical physics to much of ordinary experience, while David Hume not only drove this point home, but also revealed the repugnance of theological rationalism to the progress of experimental reasoning. In France, Rousseau declared that it was not necessary in practical affairs to follow the external sanctions of legal precedent; a more rational system of legislation than the existing one could be framed by the free decision of autonomous human wills. The crucial importance of Immanuel Kant's thought for Schleiermacher and his con-

[16] *Briefe*, v. 4, p. 45.

temporaries lay in the fact that Kant had something like a universal grasp of these changes taking place piecemeal in many minds, and was the first to suggest a program of philosophic reconstruction appropriate to the situation as a whole. For instance, in Rousseau's attitude toward legislation he saw the general conception of reason as an active principle progressing in the light of its own intrinsic ideals, and it was this conception which he placed at the center of his program. Do not look for reason in some external structure of the physical world or of traditional practices and beliefs, but dare to trust the inner reason active in producing these structures, which knows it can produce better ones.

There was no difficulty in Schleiermacher's choice between Kant and Leibniz. It would have been virtually impossible for him, or for any contemporary with similar interests and education, to prefer the traditional Leibnizean system. He might possibly appreciate the true greatness of its mathematical inventions, the refined elegance of its theology, and the humane purpose of its legal erudition, but he could no longer regard these qualities as the primary requisites of philosophy. When Schleiermacher left the University of Halle, in the eventful year of 1789, although he was fundamentally interested in religion and planned to enter the ministry, he could associate many of Leibniz's refined disquisitions with the "theological rubbish" he had left behind in the Moravian seminary. Mathematics appealed to him as a pastime. In fits of depression, he says he liked "to lose himself in resolving algebraic formulas or in geometric demonstrations."[17] How different from Leibniz, who says he

[17] *Briefe*, v. 4, p. 25.

found himself in mathematics![18] Equally great was the contrast in their attitudes toward the law. For Leibniz the development of jurisprudence seemed an all-important means of abolishing the social anarchy of his day, whereas Schleiermacher's deepest interest in the growth of a freer human culture with finer and wider feeling for the varied whole of life fed chiefly upon literary and historical materials, leading him into a region of mind beyond law, where legalistic thinking of the most delicate kind seemed too inflexible and coarse.

This was the region inhabited by whatever reason was active, not only within Schleiermacher, but also in the minds of his young contemporaries, Friedrich Schlegel, Schelling, and Hegel, who were to make the German philosophy of the future. All these young men, who, in the same decade began their intellectual careers with the study of ancient Greek civilization, were essentially interested, like Schleiermacher, in the making of a richer modern culture. Naturally they welcomed the Kantian suggestion to reconstruct philosophy in the light of an active inner reason. At the same time, Kant's ideas needed much readjustment and revision to suit their purposes.

For Kant's conception of reason, while it looked beyond the rationalities of the past, was still largely legalistic in character. He took the physics, the theology, and the law of his time as unfinished in substance, to be sure, but nevertheless as perfect in type, and he thought of his free inner reason as conquering new fields of knowledge by casting new materials into

[18] See his letter to Remond de Montmort, 1714, quoted in Ueberweg's *History of Philosophy*.

molds of this same type. This is most clearly apparent when one examines his own ventures into the newer branches of science, for instance, in biology, in history, and also in esthetics. In history and esthetics he is strong in the making of general distinctions, in legislating a scheme of interpretation, but often weak in his specific intuitions. In biology he stuck to the hypothesis of fixed forms; in reviewing Herder's *Ideas for a Philosophy of Human History*, a work of great imagination published in 1784, he speaks of evolution as "an idea from which reason shrinks back as meaningless."[19] Kant followed the trend of events assiduously, especially the progress of intellectual matters, but he could not, in a rapidly differentiating world, keep abreast of his contemporaries in everything, to say nothing of foreseeing the vast changes that were to come in the nineteenth century. Still less could he appreciate the revolution in spirit and sentiment involved by these changes, the variety of passionate idealisms which they engendered. He harbored the eighteenth century suspicion of enthusiasts. In morals he was an enlightened puritan, inasmuch as he exalted humanity and believed in freeing morality from external sanctions, whether legal or religious or even natural, but he was a puritan still, for he attributed absolute worth to nothing in man save the moral will, and relegated all other idealisms, whether esthetic, political, intellectual, or religious to a distinctly second place. His conception of right human relations was still based largely on notions of natural and civil law, ideas of contract and obligation, and he tried to

[19] Immanuel Kant, *Rezensionen von J. G. Herders Ideen zur Philosophie der Geschichte der Menschheit. Teil 1.* See also E. Adickes, *Kant als Naturforscher*, vol. ii, pp. 433-445, §328.

sum up the essence of morality in terms of obedience to a supreme law or rigidly stated principle. His practical social ideal was the realization of a universal system of civil law, which would eliminate the reign of arbitrary force between states. His theology left the rationalistic conception of Providence and immortality virtually untouched, his reforms in this field being confined to an attempt at preventing theological concepts from encroaching on the legitimate province of natural science, by insisting that the right to religious belief is in its nature moral and not theoretic.

In brief, though Kant himself called his conception of reason revolutionary, he scarcely realized the nature and extent of the revolution in which it was implicated. Not only was the claim of physics and theology to dominate over philosophy, challenged by his ideas, but the field was thrown open for every kind of wisdom that offered to satisfy a human appeal. And since modern society had developed to a point where the life it offered seemed teeming with various appeals, this invitation to develop a richer philosophy was enthusiastically welcomed. It was not long before philosophers had written metaphysics, not only in terms of the great and universal interests of mankind, such as science, art, and religion, but also in terms of every whim, all sorts of social institutions, and the traditions of the past as well. The nineteenth century saw the birth of a new industrial world, a new chemical, biological, and historical world, the making of new nations and empires. Few people could contemplate the spectacle of these changes with a dry Kantian rationality. Romanticism was a kind of spiritual quicksilver in minds that rushed to possess all this new treasure, without being themselves thoroughly possessed by any part of it. It was inevitable that this type of mind, aflame with new truths, should be the quickest to appreciate the liberation from previous dogmatisms involved in Kantian philosophy. And so it happened that Kant's most enthusiastic followers became his most radical transformers. For a brief period they poured their rich vision into gorgeous poetry and great imaginative syntheses of idealistic metaphysics. What Kant had intended as a new philosophy of the advancing critical spirit was thus speedily converted, by the romantic temper of the times, into a philosophy of the all-inclusive, appreciative, and creative spirit.

This tendency to welcome, but at the same time to revise Kant's ideas, so as to include values neglected by him, makes itself manifest from the start in Schleiermacher's relations to Kantian philosophy. There are some manuscripts dating from 1789 to 1794, the years in which, after leaving the University, he was first coming to independent grips with philosophy, and in them one may see how his thought starts from Kantian ideas and moves away from them in a direction of his own.[20] He agrees with Kant in rejecting hedonism, but he wants a richer morality than that summed up in obedience to the categorical imperative. Kant himself admits that such obedience may well fall short of achieving the *summum bonum*, and it seems unreasonable to Schleiermacher that the cardinal principle of morality should be indifferent to any of the chief goods of life. (The relation between

[20] See Appendix, pp. 115-123 for a more detailed account of these early essays. Cf. also *Dilthey*, pp. 36-152; N. E. 48-188 in connection with pp. xxxi-xxxv of the present text.

the moral law and the *summum bonum*, he thinks, should be like that between an algebraic equation and the geometrical curve described in accordance with it.)[21] In place of Kant's idea of duty he seeks a certain ideal sense of life (*eine gewisse Idealempfindung des Lebens*), which shall embrace a harmonious development of all distinctively human powers, doing justice to the intellectual, volitional and emotional sides of man's nature. In regard to religion Schleiermacher agrees with Kant in wanting to keep theological concepts out of natural science, but he feels the religious life to be something more than a belief in the tenets of Deistic Christianity for morality's sake. As one who had been "nursed in the womb of piety,"[22] he associated a strong sense of the divine presence with religion. This sense he missed in Kant's philosophy, but found in greater measure in Spinoza. Spinoza at least did justice to religious consciousness on one side by the sublime way in which he conceived the universe as a definitely ordered and unified whole, but on the other hand, Spinoza's system violated the sense of human personality. For in Spinozistic metaphysics to be an individual means to be limited; each individual is but a small fragment of nature, and can achieve true dignity only by transcending his individuality through intellectual comprehension of the universe. Schleiermacher's fundamental problem is to find a world view which does justice to human personality on the one hand, and to the infinite universe that stands over against man on the other. He wants the

[21] See below pp. 116-117.
[22] *On Religion*, p. 9.

advantages of both Kantian and Spinozistic metaphysics, of freedom and determinism.[23]

The ideas of these early papers point directly to Schleiermacher's mature works the *Speeches on Religion*, 1799, and the *Soliloquies*, 1800. In fact, when he came to review his own spiritual development in the *Soliloquies*, he saw fit to quote whole pages almost word for word from some of these early papers. At the same time there is a vast difference between Schleiermacher's work in 1793, at twenty-four years of age, and his work in 1799, at thirty, a difference like that between a honeycomb when it is empty and when it is full.[24] In 1793 he is quick in the analysis of ideas, in stating his objections and to a certain extent his objectives abstractly; in 1799 his own point of view has been filled out with experience and self-assurance. In Schleiermacher's case a certain abstract intellectual grasp of romantic principles preceded the actual substantial flowering of the romantic spirit itself. The first twenty years of his life were devoted almost entirely to study, and were quite restricted in their personal contacts. Of course he had a few friends, but being naturally shy and retiring he had no knowledge of the world, no taste of the satisfactions which varied and extensive society can bring. Speaking of the time from 1789 to 1791, which he spent at his uncle's home in the little town of Drossen, he says, "In quiet solitude I watched the great ferments of the inner and the outer world" (Kantianism and the French Revolution).[25] His manner of life developed in him a fine critical and appreciative fac-

[23] See below pp. 119-123.
[24] *Ibid.*, pp. 123-130.
[25] *Ibid.*, pp. 74-75.

ulty, but he missed the spiritual support of positive experience. He was often depressed, as many of his letters show. He found it necessary "to strengthen his heart" daily by reading from the satirists, ancient and modern cynics like Lucian, Montaigne and Wieand. He was uncertain as to his vocation, drifting toward the ministry, yet feeling that "the world will remain ever as it is, nor will morals and religion accomplish anything on the whole." In letters to his friend Brinkmann, an avowed cynic, he came to the point of discussing the merits of suicide. A slight touch of disillusionment took a permanent place in Schleiermacher's character. Even after he attained a fresh grip on himself, and other qualities came to the fore, his friends would sometimes see in him *"den klugen Schleier"* (the satirical Schleier), " and God knows what rather than the real Schleier."[26]

The initial forces that lifted Schleiermacher from this depression were not philosophical, but personal. In 1790, after passing the examinations which entitled him to preach, he accepted a position as tutor in the family of Count Dohna. This family had its estates at Schlobitten in East Prussia, was of the old nobility, and active in public affairs. "In a stranger's home," says Schleiermacher, "my sense for the beauty of human fellowship was first awakened; I saw that it takes freedom to ennoble and give right expression to the delicate intimacies of human nature."[27] Here, too, he had his first experience of love, in the form of a silent passion for a younger daughter of the Count. He began to get his *Idealempfindung des Lebens*.

[26] See *Briefe*, v. 4, pp. 27, 29, 39, 42, from which the quotations above are chosen.
[27] See below p. 74.

From 1793-'96 there followed upon these years at Schlobitten a valuable experience of teaching and preaching, first in Berlin at one of the large schools for orphans, and then at Landsberg, where he took up his first charge as a preacher. So successful was Schleiermacher in these posts that in 1796 he was given an appointment as chaplain for the Reformed Confession in a large Berlin hospital, the Charité. Here in Berlin from 1796-1802 he finally came into immediate personal contact with the larger intellectual currents of the time, meeting men whose minds were working along lines similar to those in which his own thought was half-articulately moving.

For while Schleiermacher was slowly ripening in experience during these years, the romantic spirit, of which his spirit was a part, had already received immortal expression in the work of his contemporaries. As early as 1773 Goethe had published his *Götz von Berlichingen*, and in 1774 had spread the romantic gospel far and wide in his moving description of *The Sorrows of Young Werther*. The first part of *Faust* appeared in 1790. In the '90's too Fichte began to proclaim a new idealism; in 1792 his *Critique of Religious Revelations* appeared, in 1794 his *Foundations of the Theory of Knowledge*, in 1796 his *System of Natural Right*, in '97 his *First Introduction to the Science of Knowledge*. In Goethe the consciousness of life's varied fullness produced an infinite succession of dramatic and poetic images, in which the whole slumbering world of romanticism seemed suddenly to awake. From Fichte there came no such stream of images. In him this entire world seemed to concentrate its force in the channel of moral pressure. The

Kantian revolution, as he interpreted it, meant to replace the stagnant moralities of law and convention by the infinite energizing of an inwardly moral will. In Goethe and Fichte romanticism had found its poet and its prophet.[28]

As is usually the case, the new gospel was born in the quiet freedom of the provinces, and only gradually took possession of the great capitals where the existing order was naturally strongest. The first great works of romantic literature, fresh, strong, and honest in their feeling for a larger and more varied world than that of eighteenth century conventions, were conceived in Strassburg, Jena, and Weimar. In Strassburg, where the mediaeval spirit lingered in the vastness of its cathedral, and where the contrast of French and German character suggested distinctions other than those of law and convention; in Jena and Weimar, where the political element was in the diminutive and even the Prince not only had interest, but time for poetry and science. In the provinces Goethe's glorification of the lawless knight in *Götz* and of the idle lover in *Werther*, and Schiller's eulogy of *The Robbers* could be conceived. But in the metropolis of Berlin the spirit of law and of rationalistic enlightenment still persisted; until 1786 in fact it was enthroned in the person of the "philosopher-king" himself, Frederick the Great of Prussia. Here was the seat of orderly government, and here an active group of popular philosophers and journalists, like Nicolai, turned rationalistic thought into a praise of civic virtue. But here too, as in every large city, were splendid opportunities for a more daring sort of parlor intellectualism. Into this

[28] *Dilthey*, pp. 155-182; N. E. 191-218.

medium the new literature of romanticism came like an electric shock. The manner of the idle lover *Werther* was discussed and adopted and became a self-conscious fashion, all the more because of the contrasted commercial and political spirit of the town.[29]

The salon Schleiermacher most frequented was that of the brilliant Madame Herz; here he met Friedrich Schlegel in 1797. Thereafter, half the day, he says, was spent in reading, chatting, and walking with Schlegel and Madame Herz, and his greatest joy would have been to spend more time this way. For, "Leisure was his gracious goddess. She teaches man to know and to confirm himself."[30] Schlegel and Schleiermacher both shared the general enthusiasm for the new spirit, and in particular they met on the common ground of an interest in the Greek classics. They became close friends, and for a while roomed together. Schleiermacher was the more reserved, the more careful, critical, dependable, and persevering of the two, Schlegel the more mature, enterprising, and imaginative. Although he was little older than Schleiermacher, he had already made an impression as an author, and had an ambitious program of production. He aspired to out-Goethe Goethe and out-Fichte Fichte. He would revolutionize taste and morals by the criticism of history, by putting before the narrow, conventional public mind the whole gamut of human nature as revealed in its infinitely varied manifestations. He would add to this imaginative sketches and romances, portraying possible forms of humanity as yet unrealized. (His brother William had projected and begun translations

[29] *Dilthey*, pp. 182-194; N. E. 218-230.
[30] See below, p. 36, *Soliloquies*, and cf. *Letters*, v. 1, p. 170, and p. 268.

of Cervantes, of Dante, of Shakespeare, and of Hindu classics—all admirably suited to his program.) Schlegel gathered about himself a group of young intellectuals, among them Tieck, Novalis, and Schleiermacher.[31] Together they published *The Athenaeum* (from 1798-1800), a journal devoted to spreading "the real romanticism." They looked upon the work of Goethe and Fichte as impressive and invaluable, but still as somewhat coarse-grained. Fichte's ethics, for example, did not show enough appreciation of individual differences. In later years an English critic, having large contrasts in mind, spoke of Goethe as the great opponent of Philistinism, but in those years Novalis could say, as a member of the inner romantic circle: Goethe is impossibly bourgeois.[32] When one compares the names of literary characters created by Goethe, such as Gretchen, Wilhelm Meister, Werther, with those more favored by the "real romanticists," for instance, Julian, Florentin, Hyperion, Thalia, Evremont, Woldemar, and Hyacinth, one gets an inkling of what is meant. This latter group of characters and their authors represent the interest in variety and imagination grown fastidious, delicate, extravagant, doctrinnaire, self-conscious, refined, and volatile, saturating every atom of existence with its essence.

Two salient facts, aside from qualities of personal character, set off Schleiermacher from the rest of this romantic group, and made his position in it somewhat anomalous. In the first place, he was a preacher by profession, whereas most of the others inclined to identify religion, especially the church, with the old

[31] See *Dilthey*, pp. 194-296ff.; N. E. 230-331, in re the Berlin romanticists.
[32] Novalis, *Schriften*, v. 2, pp. 68ff.

INTRODUCTION xxxix

order and its cultural limitations. In the second place, he had no marked literary gift, while the essential medium of the group's activity was literary. Schleiermacher was extremely conscious that both of these circumstances were deeply rooted in his character, and must have felt that if he was to maintain his position in the group he had to show at least that they were no obstacle. Schlegel was forever prodding him to write something, but could get nothing from him except short contributions to the *Athenaeum*. Finally, in 1797, on Schleiermacher's birthday, he extracted a promise of something more ambitious.[83] The result was the beginning next year of a work *On Religion: Speeches addressed to its cultured despisers*. By the cultured despisers of religion were meant pre-eminently Schleiermacher's fellow romanticists, whom he undertook to show that a true love of life's fullness and variety would make them friendly to religion. This was followed in 1800 by the *Soliloquies*, meditations on the more intimate and personal question of his own inner nature and its relations to his friends. Herein he argued that even without producing works, for instance, literary works, he might still find his salvation in the romantic faith alone.

Both the *Speeches* and the *Soliloquies* are thus apologetic in motive, but by virtue of their substance they belong to that class of apologies which sum up and modify the ideas, not of single individuals merely, but of the universal mind.[84] The *Speeches on Religion* appeared first in 1799, and it was in part his enthusi-

[83] *Letters,* v. 1, p. 163. Also see *Dilthey,* pp. 235-236; N. E. 271-272.
[84] *Dilthey,* pp. 297-508; N. E. 331-551 for the *Reden* and *Monologen*.

asm over their successful completion that led Schleiermacher so quickly to the publication of a second work, the *Soliloquies* in 1800. But much of this second work was really conceived earlier than the *Speeches*, and in a fundamental sense presupposed by them, as an author's life is always presupposed in his works, for the theme of the *Soliloquies* is that of Schleiermacher's own spiritual development, and whole sections of the work are virtually quoted word for word from essays in manuscript and from sermons dating from the years of his philosophic awakening 1789-1793.[35] As a contributor to the *Athenaeum* Schleiermacher had long planned to develop the ideas of these early essays into something like a formal polemic against Kantian-Fichtean ethics. At the same time he was tempted by the example of his colleagues, Schlegel, Tieck and others, to try his hand at more fanciful forms of writing, and for a time played with the idea of a romantic novel embodying his ethical views.[36] His sensitive imagination and his strong critical bent were forever at war over the choice of a literary medium. Finally in 1799, the successful completion of his *Speeches on Religion* (a form of literary expression in which preaching had made him competent) gave him greater poise and self-confidence. On the evening of his birthday, a few months later, he wrote to his sister: "I wish you could share the quiet joy which possesses my soul. I rejoice over the past, and for the present, and I look with equanimity toward the future, whatever it may bring. I can say with reasonable certainty that this will be my ruling mood as long as I live, for

[35] See below p. 118 and note.
[36] See below p. 88 and note. And also *Dilthey*, pp. 289-296; N. E. 323-331.

INTRODUCTION xli

it is grounded in my inmost self."[37] In this spirit of self-possession, and of happy reminiscence, the idea of the *Soliloquies* seems to have suggested itself to Schleiermacher, a series of meditations dealing with the problems of his inner life, as the *Speeches* had just dealt with the fundamental problems underlying his public vocation as a preacher. The idea took possession of him, and he completed the *Soliloquies* in less than four weeks, virtually "dictating it to the printer," he says. He was able to do this, because he took the idea of soliloquy seriously, and felt singularly free to follow his spontaneous impulses. He put in extracts from his early papers, bits of polemic against popular rationalism, against Kant and Fichte, personalia and philosophy just as the spirit moved him. He indulged his literary conceit by casting the whole into a kind of effusive rhythmic prose. The result cannot be called very happy from the point of view of construction and style, but as a revelation of his spirit and its romantic milieu it could scarcely be surpassed. To Henrietta Herz he happily spoke of the book as "a lyric extract from the diary of his abiding self."[38]

There are five soliloquies or meditations, and the first is on the general theme of meditation itself. Schleiermacher considers the different ways in which people introspect and take account of themselves and their lives. There are the people who sit down on New Year's Day,[39] or at some other time appointed

[37] *Letters*, v. 1, pp. 227-228.
[38] See Schiele's introduction to the *Monologen* (*Schiele*, pp. xiv-xxxv) for these quotations and much else of interest regarding the origin of the *Soliloquies*.
[39] Schleiermacher had preached on this New Year's Day theme in 1792, and the sermon contains many ideas later developed more fully in the *Soliloquies*. Cf. p. 12 and note.

by mere convention, to review the joys and sorrows of the past, or to count up their achievements and shortcomings. Such people are slaves to circumstance, because they look at life, even their own lives, from the outside. They naturally think of the world as the primary reality, and of life as a series of temporal experiences taking place in the world. Either they try to dwell on the particular experiences which satisfy them most, while time relentlessly sweeps them on, or they set up an external ideal of perfection, a God above the world and an immortal blessedness after death. Their's is the popular rationalism of the age, which finds reason essentially in the external facts of nature and of convention. How different from the meditations of "these children of the age" are those of the man for whom the spirit within himself and in others and in the world is the primary reality! For him circumstances are but the occasions and the materials through which the spirit manifests itself. In the consciousness of a spiritual nature, and of opportunities everywhere present for its exercise, he has an unfailing sense of his freedom, and feels himself to be in immediate contact with the Infinite and Eternal, partaking of God and immortality in every moment.

The second soliloquy leaves the empiricist behind, and treats in autobiographical terms of Schleiermacher's own discoveries in the realm of spirit. First, the awakening of a sense of the ideal possibilities of human life is described in language suggesting that of religious conversion. The sense of exalted assurance which this awakening gives is contrasted with the pitiable squirming of the unconverted human before his conscience. Conscience is generally a distorted form of ideal consciousness, the ideal turned prison-warden of the self. This description of conscience is the first note in a new polemic now introduced against Kant and Fichte. The moral life as they picture it is life lived in the light of a universal reason, the same for every one. But, penetrating more deeply into the realm of spirit, Schleiermacher discovers a higher law of individuation. Each human being has his own unique place within the sphere of humanity, and it is only by his approaching this that he can exercise his influence in the spiritual community. This discovery leads to the theme of human variety, of Schleiermacher's own character and its relation to that of his friends, his convictions and remaining uncertainties. He divides humanity into two large groups, according to whether the productive or the receptive impulse predominates. He places himself in the latter group, protesting to his artist friends that they should not urge him to produce works. Let them recognize that it is as truly an art to mold one's own nature as to mold words and sounds. The problems of the receptive spirit are discussed, its requirements, and its genius for sympathetic understanding in love and friendship. But there is a note of uncertainty throughout. Schleiermacher protests too much, and later, in the fourth soliloquy, when he returns to autobiography, confesses his hankering to pour the whole essence of his nature into a novel.[40]

The third soliloquy contrasts two ideals of civilization, showing how the empirical and the spiritual viewpoints lead to two different conceptions of humanity's task on earth. For the former, progress tends to be

[40] See below p. 88 and note.

measured in terms of man's control over nature; human co-operation, as in the economic division of labor, is directed toward this end. At most, men help each other to be happy. But the pursuit of higher, spiritual interests, in the present state of human development, each soul must conduct alone? Where is the art of fellowship and association in these matters? "Whatever spiritual association now exists is debased in service of the earthly."[41] Friendship, marriage, and the state, when not viewed as means to individual pleasure, are ordinarily regarded with reference to some other external function, but very rarely as distinct forms of spiritual life. Just as the present dominion of man over nature was undreamed of by primitive man, so are we blind to the possibilities of spiritual society. But here and there the inner glow of a better future appears in the words and actions of some individual. As soon, however, as his precious accents and manners are recognized by others, and become current, the danger arises that they be imitated and debased by worldlings. True inwardness, true spirituality, must ever be won anew. Man belongs to the world he helps to create; and so Schleiermacher and his romantic friends are strangers to the crude present, prophet-children of a better time.

The fourth soliloquy asks for assurance as to the future, and faces the problem of destiny. The answer is that freedom hinges on self-determination of the proper kind. As long as one seeks some particular external disposition of things, the future must seem uncertain, the problems of casuistry and magic are vital. One wants to know whether the outward pow-

[41] See below p. 56.

ers are arbitrary or providential. But as soon as one accepts the task of self-culture, and keeps the whole of its implications before the mind, all fear vanishes, for every circumstance, whatever it be, is an opportunity toward such an ideal. "The spirit can find no evil in anything that merely changes its activity from one form to another."[42] The theme now returns to autobiography. Schleiermacher reviews the results of the past for his own self-culture, and outlines the opportunities which remain for him in the future. But what if fate should rob him of these?—the main question is raised again. For instance, suppose he should be obliged to leave Berlin, in the midst of his scientific and cultural interests, and go to some small, unlettered province. Imagination will then supply the absent goods. He applies this solution even to his hope of marriage—if his beloved is denied him, he will live with her in imagination! "In the future as in the past I shall take possession of the whole world by virtue of inner activity."[43] Here one sees clearly the interdependence in romanticist philosophy of its characteristic inwardness and its desire for a rich, varied experience. Everything attracts the romanticist; if he cannot have one thing he will fall in love with another, and what he cannot have in fact he will have in imagination. It does not much matter what particular items fall into these two classes; hence the confusion of categories, hence the indifference to the distinction between fact and fancy. The reality of the imagined, in a sophisticated, critical mind, hinges on the fact that one wants so many and such choice things, that one can have them only in imagination.

[42] See below p. 94.   [43] See below p. 82.

The last soliloquy is a beautiful rhapsody on the way the life of spirit should be lived. The contrast between youth and age furnishes the underlying motif. For the empiricist this is a temporal contrast; life is fresh and young at the start, and when youth is spent, then follows old age, dry and stiff, though not without its crown of virtues. For the spiritual eye, however, youth and age are two eternal principles, two deities, and in their early marriage in the human soul lies the secret of spiritual strength. The *Soliloquies* close with a picture of this strength: let your inmost self be ever young, tender, plastic, impressionable, forever growing and blooming, but let what you offer to the world be always sound fruit, ripened and well-seasoned in the cool deliberation of mature wisdom.

The *Soliloquies* reveal the tender, plastic center of Schleiermacher's spirit, its eternal youthfulness and immaturity. But his *Speeches on Religion*, published a year earlier, had shown that he could produce sound fruit also.[44] In every way they are a firmer work, better-seasoned in judgment and harder in expression. Yet they are work of the same man and the same spirit, only deployed not on the tender center of his own personality, but more objectively on the segment of life in which he was most deeply interested, religion. He undertakes a defence of religion, of Christianity and the church too, which in his view have all been misunderstood and depreciated because of the prevalence of popular rationalism and externalist philosophy.

"The children of the age," these externalists, are niggardly minds: everything must be plain to them.

[44] Cf. pp. 98-99 below and note.

They believe that their conventions embrace the sphere of humanity, and that if others would only be enlightened and do as they do, no consciousness of further possibilities would be necessary. "They trim everything with their own shears, and will not suffer anything unusual, that might awaken a religious interest, to show its head. What can be seen and understood from their standpoint is all that they allow, and it is merely a small, waste land without science, without manners, without art, without love, without spirit, I might almost say without literacy; in short, lacking everything whereby one can get hold of reality. But these very people lay high claim to all these possessions. The believe they have the true reality, and that they alone see all things in their right relations. . . . For humanity in its present environment there are certain windows open to the Infinite, hewn-out casements, past which every man is led in order that his sensibility may find a way to the great All. The prospects from these casements, while they may not produce religious feelings of a definite character, may still awaken a general susceptibility to religion. Hence these outlets are also prudently stopped up by the worldly-wise, and some caricature of philosophy is stood up in the opening. . . . Birth and death are such outlets. In their presence it is impossible to forget that our own selves are completely surrounded by the Infinite. Despite their frequency, as soon as they touch us nearly, they always cause an inner pang and a holy reverence. The immeasurability of sense perception is also a hint at least of a still higher infinity. But nothing would better please those men of worldly wisdom than to be able to measure the universe. And, if the images of life and death approach them, believe me, however much they may speak of religion, they are much more concerned to use the occasion for winning their young to a cautious economy in the interest of prolonging life. This is the extreme of utilitarianism, and its punishment is to move slavishly in ancient forms of wisdom and to achieve improvements only in the lower aspects of life. It is enlightened barbarism, a fit counterpart for the old."[45]

The only religion these enlightened barbarians will allow is what they call natural or rational religion, a patchwork they have put together of pieces cut out of their metaphysics, their ethics, and their religious tradition. But the fact that they can regard their ethics and metaphysics as rational shows the superficiality of their intellectualism. And their willingness to call this artificial construction of theirs a religion proves their utter lack of religious feeling. If this is to be the religion of modern times, the truly cultured are right in abandoning it and turning to atheism. For in their atheism they show more feeling for the Infinite than popular rationalism does in its religion.[46]

True religion is not a "patchwork of ethical and metaphysical crumbs," but "a sense and taste for the Infinite."[47] It neither begins nor ends with theology, but with a wider sense of our spiritual atmosphere, of the conditions and the possibilities with which infinite being surrounds us. Science strives for an understanding of the universe, but religion seeks to adjust the very roots of our being, our feelings and actions

[45] *On Religion*, pp. 129-131.
[46] See *On Religion*, pp. 27ff., 214, 230ff. in re "natural religion."
[47] *On Religion*, pp. 31, 39.

as well as our ideas, to the whole in which we are placed. It is the making of a universe out of the objective and the subjective, in which our whole being has its life. Two great spiritual tendencies combine in religion, the one toward individuality or uniqueness of soul and the other toward universality or fullness of soul.[48] Man is sensitive and responsive to a great variety of influences, peculiarly fitted to draw nourishment from the universe, and whatever he assimilates is thereby transformed and given a new significance; it enters a new unity, the artistic and purposeful unity of a personality. Through fullness of thought and action, and by wide receptivity to impressions of every kind the human individual gains a cosmic outlook, and at the same time enhances his individuality. By receiving the universe into his soul, he becomes, as it were, the soul of a second universe where the planets move in communion with him, and where his individuality enters into the life of all. The universe itself acquires a kind of infinity through being thus received in individual souls, as if it were reflected and reflected again in an infinite series of different mirrors.

Not to theology, which is but one aspect of religion, but to this making of worlds in which the human spirit is at home, Schleiermacher invites his romanticist friends. Here in the sphere of religion, he tells them, they will find the greatest scope for their love of individuation, variety, and fullness. Science, morals, and art all have their special functions and limitations, but religion is the domain of pure spirituality in its immediacy and totality. These other activities are responsible for the definite solution of specific problems

[48] Cf. below pp. 127-128.

in theory and in practice, but religion lifts her eyes from the immediate scene or the immediate work toward the ultimate beginnings and fruitions of life. It adds depth, intensity, and fullness to our otherwise thin experience. "Let no one turn from religion for the sake of his spiritual independence," says Schleiermacher. It is not the possession of a sacred book, but an original and living understanding thereof that characterizes a truly religious spirit, not theology but theologizing. He was a more religious man who could make a Bible than he who reveres one."[49]

Well might Pope Pius X, in condemning modernism, warn the faithful that this philosophy of religion opened wide the door to individual religion![50] That it should do so was one of Schleiermacher's most fervent wishes. The true church, he says, has ever existed as a free communion between all truly religious spirits wherever they may be. "And the visible religious society can only be brought nearer the universal freedom and majestic unity of a true church by becoming a mobile mass, having no distinct outlines, each part being now here, now there, and all peacefully mingling together. . . . According to the principles of the true church, the mission of the priest in the world is a private one, and the temple should also be a private chamber where he lifts up his voice to give utterance to religion. Let there be a gathering before him and not a congregation. Let him be a speaker for all who will hear, but not a shepherd for a definite flock. . . . Nay, finally in the development of culture, we expect a time when no other society

[49] *On Religion*, pp. 90-91.
[50] See the famous encyclical, *Pascendi gregis*.

will be required for religious teaching except a religious family life."[51]

But in this future age of free religious association and development what will become of the great world religions as we know them today? One might suppose that Schleiermacher with his extreme emphasis on individual religion would have little use for the great traditions of Judaism and Christianity and Mohammedanism. But such an impression he associates with the false view of popular rationalism that individuality means isolation. On the contrary, he says, individuation is not by exclusion, but by manifold relation; it involves innumerable organic filaments, among them historic connections, which only those who do not understand it can wish to destroy. "And just as no man can reach his fulfillment as an individual without in the process finding himself placed in a world with manifold relations to other objects and to a definite order of things, so no man can attain his religious individuation without thereby finding himself in a communion, that is, in a definite form of religion."[52] Within the universal realm of religion there are different provinces distinguished from each other by many specific circumstances that bear an important relation to individual development. Judaism and Christianity are such provinces, distinguished among other ways by the fact that different religious emotions are dominant in each. Judaism is permeated everywhere by the desire for justification, Christianity by the desire for redemption. Such differences of

[51] *On Religion,* pp. 175, 178.
[52] *On Religion,* p. 230.

emotional complex are for Schleiermacher the most crucial differentia of the religions.[53]

The *Speeches on Religion* close with an appreciation of Christianity. Whoever feels with Christ that everything "finite requires a higher mediation to be in accord with the Deity, and that for man in bondage to the finite and particular, all too ready to imagine the divine itself in this form, salvation is only to be found in redemption, whoever has this sense of the divine and feels this need of redemption as the cardinal point in his religious consciousness is a Christian," and "when he understands the whole efficacy of Christ in the religious world, he will acknowledge Him as the true founder of redemption and reconciliation."[54] How he conceives the metaphysical status of Christ is an entirely secondary matter. As ministering to the need for redemption, Christianity will yet have a long history. But will it become universal and exist as the sole type of religion? It scorns the thought of being so restrictive and despotic. Christ never said that his religious views and feelings expressed the whole of man's relations to the Eternal. Christianity is essentially polemic, deeply conscious that the Perfect is infinite and hence that all finite religion, including itself, is inadequate and imperfect. It is full of sorrow, and it is everlastingly warring against the world, even against its own members inasmuch as they too are of the world. "No religion is so completely filled as Christianity with the yeast of idealization, none does so take up the challenge of an everlasting war to purify the actual, a task which never can be

[53] *On Religion*, pp. 222ff., 238ff. Cf. below pp. 155-157.
[54] *On Religion*, pp. 246, 248.

consummated."[55] "And hence this religion of religions longs to see the ideal forces of Humanity aspiring to infinity. From its own life it is ever sending forth new variations in the effort to express its essence still more purely and completely," and "it willingly sees other and younger, and, if possible, stronger and more beautiful types of religion arise outside of it. It cannot find enough ways of expressing its pure devotion to all things human. And as nothing is more irreligious than to demand a general uniformity among all men, so nothing is more unchristian than to seek uniformity in religion. The deity is to be contemplated and worshipped in all ways."[56] For the universe is infinite and its life can only be sensed through infinite individuation.

How different this romantic appreciation of the great religious traditions is from the single-minded allegiance of an undivided faith, by which the devout are admonished ever to repeat the words: "I am naught, I have naught, I desire naught, but to be in Jerusalem."[57] By way of contrast, here is the romanticist desiring to be in Jerusalem, but everywhere else at the same time. The latter's spirituality is the kind that generally pervades "modernism," forward-looking, backward looking, looking to every side, upward, and perhaps sometimes downward. It is a sensitive and generous spirituality, but through lack of concentration, its direction from time to time is apt to be determined by extrinsic forces and circumstances.

This is not the place to discuss the permanent value of romantic spirituality in the world's pantheon of re-

[55] *On Religion*, p. 243.
[56] *On Religion*, p. 252.
[57] Walter Hilton, *Parable of the Pilgrim*.

ligions. There will always be some who prefer another type of religious sentiment and still others who prefer none at all. But for those who are interested in romantic religion the latter half of Schleiermacher's life, the fate of his ideas and their influence, contains some illuminating experience. For a brief while after the publication of the *Speeches on Religion* he and his fellow romanticists indulged the hope of founding a new religion or at least of inaugurating a new religious awakening. The circumstances of the time seemed favorable to change; there was the example of the French revolution. But almost at once these grandiose ambitions were deflected by the complications of more personal romantic longings. Schlegel and Schleiermacher both fell in love with married women; Schleiermacher refrained from forcing his lady's hand (and several years later she finally rejected him definitely),[58] but Schlegel eloped with Dorothea Veit. Although Schleiermacher did not approve, he defended his friend against the storm of criticism that followed, thereby drawing upon himself some of its force. The strained personal relations that ensued led to the dispersal of the romantic group. Schlegel went to Jena, while the church found a position for Schleiermacher as court-preacher at Stolpe, a small town in Pommerania.[59] Here he stayed from 1802 to 1804, and during his exile turned his attention to exacting scholarship, continuing the translation of Plato's Dialogues which he had begun with Schlegel, and writing out the *Outlines of a*

[58] See below pp. 79ff. and note †.

[59] *Dilthey*, pp. 509-542 describes these *Trennungen*. And the New Edition by Herm. Mulert, 1922, adds a very valuable section (N. E. pp. 552-861) on Schleiermacher's life from 1800-1807.

Critique of Previous Ethical Theory which he had long contemplated. This latter work shows little trace of romantic idealism; it is a stiff piece of pure logical analysis from beginning to end. (See Appendix, pp. 132-134).[60]

These scholarly labors qualified Schleiermacher for an academic post and in 1804 he accepted a professorship and chaplaincy at his former university of Halle. Here he preached and taught both philosophy and theology for about two years, at the end of which time the university had to be closed because of the French invasion of 1806. This invasion proved the weakness of the old regime in Prussia, bringing disintegration and suffering in its train, but it likewise raised new hopes of rebuilding life on a higher spiritual as well as material level. These were the days of Fichte's *Speeches to the German Nation*, the days of his greatest influence as a spiritual leader. A new university was created at Berlin to which the foremost spirits of the day were to be drawn and which was to radiate its influence throughout a new society. To this university Schleiermacher was invited to come as head of the theological faculty and in 1810 he took up his post there, and outlined his program for theological study. His *Kurze Darstellung des Theologischen Studiums* (1811) in its essential elements has been the educational program of progressive Protestant seminaries ever since. (See Appendix, pp. 149ff.) His distinguished academic post accompanied a position oi

[60] The brief sketch of Schleiermacher's life after 1800 given above is supplemented by a more detailed consideration of his later writings in the Appendix, pp. 115ff. below. See Preface, p. vi. For the second half of Schleiermacher's life see also Dilthey's article in the *Allgemeine Deutsche Biographie*.

prominence in the church. In 1808 he had been called to the important pulpit of the Dreifaltigkeits Kirche.

In the pulpit, as in the academy, Schleiermacher worked with the liberals. In ecclesiastical politics he tried to secure that most difficult of all arrangements, the widest possible cooperation of all parties on a basis of free independent expression. He was bitterly opposed to legal coercion in religious matters. ("Away with every union between church and state. That remains my Cato's utterance to the end or until I see the union actually destroyed.")[61] But in 1817 the Reformed and Lutheran Confessions were finally joined, not as Schleiermacher had hoped, by free agreement of the parties, but by pressure from the state. As the Metternich reaction intensified, Schleiermacher found himself in difficulties with the government because of his liberal views. A charge of "demagogic agitation" was issued against him and Arndt. Political reaction meant religious orthodoxy too. The growing influence of Hengstenberg, the disciplining of De Wette in 1819, meant the ascendency of everything against which Schleiermacher was contending, the rigid control of the church by the orthodox party in alliance with the reactionary state.

The times now needed a philosophy that took hold of political and social realities. The romanticists possessed considerable historical sense, but they used their knowledge of history in the service of individual rather than of social imagination, and such freely imaginative idealism, which had been the spirit of the times only a few years before, was now gradually relegated to the academy, while events took an inde-

[61] *On Religion,* p. 174.

pendent course. In the philosophic works of his later years Schleiermacher, for instance, seems largely to be engaged in the academic exercise of giving his ideas a more systematic formulation. (See Appendix, pp. 130ff.) Naturally, however, he sensed the new situation, and tried also to do justice in his later theory to the problems of institutionalized spirituality.[62] But Hegel alone of all the idealists impressed men by his profound sense of organized human life, and so Hegel succeeded the romanticists as the philosophic oracle of the hour.

Schleiermacher's philosophy in his later years was no longer an expression of the movement of things as a whole, such as it had been for a brief while at the turn of the century. But in one department of thought he continued to reap a fine harvest from his early planting. With impressive accumulative result he developed his philosophy of religion and applied it to the interpretation of Christian history and theology. His life became more and more deeply and significantly bound up with the life of the Protestant church. The results of his exegetical and historical researches have long since been superseded in many respects, but only by the more general application of those critical methods, which he was among the first to adopt. In the realm of Christian theology, too, new ideas have become current since he published his great work on *The Christian Faith (according to Evangelical Doctrine)* in 1821. But the underlying principle of this work, that systems of theology are to be understood as symbolizing religious experience, has never commanded wider respect among all the various classes

[62] Cf. below pp. 146-149.

of men interested in the interpretation of religion than today. (See Appendix, pp. 162-165.)

The question has often been raised whether Schleiermacher's theory of religion as developed in his later systematic works is consistent with his earlier ideas in the *Speeches on Religion.* There is a very fundamental difference between the two that can scarcely be described in terms of consistency or inconsistency. Considered as purely theoretical works, the earlier and later writings are on the whole harmonious, but the important point of difference is that the earlier writings were not intended as purely theoretical, like the later ones, but as something more. In them the larger purpose was active, not merely to interpret, but also to create, or at least to move men to create religion, and it is by the standard of this, his highest ambition that Schleiermacher should be judged. To interpret religion is one thing, and to create it quite another. Schleiermacher's reputation as a philosopher of religion is good, but what of his rank as a prophet?

For a brief moment, on the threshold of the nineteenth century, he and his fellow-romanticists had been in touch with the spirit of things as a whole. They caught the thrill of the larger world into which humanity was moving, and welcomed the promise of a richly varied existence with an enthusiasm that sets them apart in the history of human thought. For mankind has usually sought security in some permanent or stable fact of life, and has rarely indulged an interest, with such complete abandon as the romanticists showed, in all the variations of experience. Since 1800 we have come to know something of the pain and difficulty involved in the differentiation and complexity of modern life, so that the emotional excitement of the romanticists may appear somewhat visionary and out of touch with reality. We are impressed with the need of understanding as well as of feeling the qualities of our culture. And yet, we should be loath to forego the opportunities for individual development or the variety of values that contemporary life affords. The ideals of romanticism are still in many respects vital, although the classic philosophies of romanticism are felt to be inadequate, especially as the lyric enthusiasm of a hundred years ago will not suffice to realize these ideals under present conditions of human existence.

But can the pursuit and appreciation of the varied goods of life ever give an absolute satisfaction akin to that sought in the great religions? Can it receive an adequate social anchorage and an adequate ideal expression? This is the fundamental question raised by the strength and weakness of the romantic movement, and the life of the modern spirit is really at stake in it. For we do not wish to give up the variety of values which we enjoy, and at the same time we know that mere wishing and appreciation will not maintain them for us, because imperious forces and circumstances play havoc with us when not understood and controlled. We cannot return to the mediaeval faith, or be satisfied with any other religious view that in the light of a wider horizon seems to set up a one-sided ideal; neither can we be content with "modernism" in the sense of a mere recognition of other values, or a romantic tasting of them. Such modernism like romanticism is too optimistic about the basis on which the life of the spirit rests. It takes for granted and accepts as a matter of course dispositions and powers that have been slowly built up by constructive effort, just as romanticism took for granted the solid foundations laid for modern life and thought in the seventeenth and eighteenth centuries. Without the gradual accumulation of varied goods and powers by constructive thought and discipline, the romantic appreciation of a many-sided and rich existence would not have been possible, nor can the possibility be maintained without the transformation of appreciation from something fluidly romantic into something more organic and structural.

SCHLEIERMACHER'S SOLILOQUIES

PREFACE TO THE SECOND EDITION

WHEN THIS LITTLE BOOK went out of print, I did not wish to refuse the publication of a second edition. In part, because I am indebted to the book for attracting readers of generous spirit in a way I had hardly expected, and for bringing me highly esteemed friends.* And then also because such a refusal to reprint might be misinterpreted as a recantation. Let me, therefore, render thanks to these pages by granting them a new lease of life, at the same time explaining that all the sentiments expressed in them are still my own as fully as any portrait drawn in early life can and should resemble one's older self. But in re-editing the book I must confess that the difficulties involved in touching up a work like this, to say nothing of revising it, are all too great, because there is danger, on the one hand, of clouding its essential, inner truth by an unconscious infusion of characteristics of a later period, or on the other hand, of disturbing friendly readers by changes which might appear arbitrary. For these reasons I prefer to republish it with all its imperfections, and except in small matters of expression I have made only a few changes noted down soon after its first appearance, because they seemed to clarify some obscurities and to prevent mis-

* Among them Ehrenfried v. Willich, whose widow Schleiermacher married. See *Letters*, v. 1, p. 266ff. E. v. Willich, S.'s stepson, has given an interesting picture of the family life in *Aus Schleiermacher's Hause*.

understandings. Therefore, if anyone finds fault with the manner in which the book is written rather than with its content, let him not attribute the defect to me as I am now, but rather to the man I was when this book first appeared. But if there be others who find the very spirit of the book uncongenial, and who are unwilling or unable to distinguish between a man's ideal self and his mere appearance, nothing need hinder them from serving up again the flat and tasteless ridicule heard here and there ten years ago.*

Dr. Fr. Schleiermacher.

Berlin, April, 1810.

---

*D. F. Strauss's *Charakteristiken und Kritiken,* p. 27, questions the effectiveness of this apology and accepts Schleiermacher's invitation to criticize the *Soliloquies.*

PREFACE TO THE THIRD EDITION

IN PUBLISHING this third edition of my little book I refer the reader again to the justification given in the preface to the second edition, and shall attempt only a few additional words for the benefit of those who may have really misinterpreted what the book aims to accomplish. Since the second edition was published, an intimate friend of long acquaintance made the following very pertinent statement. The life of every individual, as it appears to others, suggests at one time his essential, archetypal self, and at another his distorted self. Now only when following out the first suggestion, that toward the archetypal self, can self-examination yield results fit for publication and communicable to others; introspection in the other direction, toward the distorted self, is soon lost too deep in those recesses of the private life which, as some sage has already said, a man had best conceal even from himself. He who passes over this latter type of introspection, as was attempted in this book, while communicating his findings in the former, obviously with the special intention of locating the points of difference between archetypal selves, is completely misinterpreted if he is censured for seeing himself only in a favorable light, and for being more ridiculous than Narcissus, in that he goes so far as to publish for the whole wide world to read the language of infatuation which he has addressed to his own likeness. Moreover, to this purpose of the book can be attributed the fact that self-examination assumes in it a purely ethical form, and that what is in a narrow sense religous should nowhere be prominent therein.* But I did not intend this to favor the view that religious introspection must tend only in the opposite direction of contemplating man's distorted, fallen self.† On the contrary, it has long been my plan to refute this one-sided conception also, and to supplement this book by a similar series of religious meditations. But thus far time has not permitted me to do so.‡

BERLIN, December, 1821. S.

* Cf. pp. xlix, 22, 127, for Schleiermacher's conception of the relations between the ethical and the religious. In a fundamental sense the *Soliloquies* concern both.
† This refers to the pietist revival (1821) of meditation upon human sinfulness. (*Schiele,* p. 95.)
‡ The plan was never carried out.

SOLILOQUIES

A

NEW YEAR'S GIFT

BERLIN 1800
PUBLISHED BY CHRISTIAN SIGISMUND SPENER

OFFERING

NO choicer[1] gift can any man give to another than his spirit's intimate converse with itself.* For this affords the highest[2] boon there is, a clear and undistorted insight into a free being. No gift is more enduring, for nothing can destroy the satisfaction, which such an insight has once granted you,[3] and its intrinsic truth assures your love so that you delight in beholding it again. None is surer proof against the lust and guile of others, since it arouses no desire that is not spiritual, and offers no secondary attractions that could lead to its abuse. If anyone stands aloof, and looks askance at this precious treasure, attributing to it absurd features which your honest eye does not detect, let not such idle mockery rob you of your joy. Heed it as little as I shall let myself repent of having shared with you that which I had to give. Come, take the gift, ye who can understand my spirit's thought![4] May my feelings here intoned be an accompaniment to the melody within yourselves, and may the shock which passes through you at the contact with my spirit, become a quickening impulse in your life.

[Note: The numerical notes refer to changes made in the text by Schleiermacher himself in the second and third editions. These changes are given on pp. 104-111.]

*That the *Soliloquies* virtually do represent Schleiermacher's inner conversation during years of growth I have explained on p. xl (Introduction). Pp. xli-xlvi give a brief analysis of the work.

I

REFLECTION

THE outer world in its eternal laws as well as in its most ephemeral appearances, like a magic mirror, doubtless reflects our highest and innermost nature in a thousand tender and sublime similitudes.* But this happy imagery, the delicate charm of which should enliven and inform dull sensibilities as it plays upon them, is of no avail to such as disregard the plain demands of their own deepest feelings and do not hear the subdued sighing of their abused spirit. The true significance and inner purport of outward relations escapes them, even of such as their own genius has contrived and must repeatedly bring to light. Thus (in the reckoning of the calendar),† we divide the infinite line of time into equal portions, at points determined arbitrarily by the most trivial circumstances, having no significance in our lives and determining nothing, since nought proceeds at an exact pace, not the structure of our work, nor the round of our emotions, nor the play of our destiny. And yet these arbitrary

* Cf. pp. 16ff. for Schleiermacher's view of the outer world in its relations to spirit. One of the recurring ideas is that the former mirrors ("symbolizes." p. 16, 146) the latter. The play upon the word "Reflection" (title) is significant and characteristic.

† The parenthetical phrase has been supplied by the translator. See note * on p. 12.

divisions are meant to be something more than an aid to the chronologer or a feast for the mathematician; to everyone they must inevitably suggest serious reflections on the possibility of dividing life. But few are they who penetrate beneath the surface of this profound allegory, and understand to what truth this very natural[5] suggestion points.

The average individual recognizes nothing but his transient existence, and its irresistible decline from sunny heights into a dread night of annihilation. He thinks some hidden hand draws the thread of his life along, alternately weaving and unweaving a web of sensations and ideas, pulling it together now loosely, now tightly, and that nothing more exists. The swifter the succession of our thoughts and feelings, the richer their variety, the more harmonious and intimate their combination, the more glorious and perfect a work of art our life is believed to be. And could men also explain in mechanistic fashion the entire nexus of such a life,[6] they would regard themselves as having reached the summit of humanity and of self-comprehension. But in thinking thus they mistake the reflected image of their activity for the whole[7] activity itself, those outer contact-points, wherein the energies of the self meet with external things, for their inmost being, they mistake the atmosphere for the world about which it has formed.* How could such men, (watching the old year out and awaiting the new), with reflections no deeper than these, understand the challenge implicit in this very act of dividing

* Cf. pp. 15-18.

time?* The point which cuts a line is not part of that line; it is related to the Infinite as truly and more immediately than to the line, and anywhere along the line you can place such a point.† Just so, the moment in which you cut the course of life and make a new division, should be no portion of your temporal existence; you should regard it otherwise, and in it become conscious of your immediate relations to the Infinite and Eternal;[8] and whenever you will, such a moment can be yours. Seeing herein a sublime intimation of the Divine in me, I rejoice in its invitation to an immortal life outside the realm of time and free from its harsh laws! But those, who do not recognize a call to this higher life, while immersed in transient thought and feeling, will equally fail to apprehend it when, without really knowing what they are about, they resort to the measurement of time for the sake of marking off periods in their mundane existence. Better that they never even suspected the truth than that their vain energetic bustle should so painfully disconcert me when I strive to obey the divine invitation! Doubtless they too demand a point in time, which shall mean more than a merely transient present, but they have not the wit to apprehend it as Eter-

---

* The *Soliloquies* are a "new year's gift" (see title-page, p. 7). The romanticists heralded the turn of the century and the advent of 1800 as the dawn of a new era. Moreover, Schleiermacher originally developed some of the themes of the *Soliloquies* in a new year's sermon of 1792 (republished in *Schiele*, p. 149). These circumstances help to explain the prominence given in the text above to the thought of the changing year and the reflections it arouses. In the interest of this thought, the parenthetical phrase above and another on p. 10, have been supplied by the translator.

† See pp. xxvii-xxviii in re Schleiermacher and mathematics!

nity. Often for a moment, sometimes perhaps for an hour or even for a day,* they will actually absolve themselves from the obligations of assiduous industry, from the eager quest for knowledge and pleasure, warned as they needs must be of the transiency of their interests, by the reflection that the present is ever slipping into the past as speedily as it emerges out of the future. There follows disillusionment and disgust with all this useless pursuit of novel enjoyments, perceptions, or activities; they sit down on the bank of the river of life, and with a helpless smile let fall their tears into the dancing waves below. Like barbarous savages who kill the wives, the children, or the slaves beside a father's grave,[9] so at the close of a departing year they sacrifice the holiday, dissipating it in empty imaginings, a thoroughly vain oblation.

Meditation and contemplation are without profit for him who does not know[10] the inner life of spirit. Let him not struggle to escape from temporal things, who recognizes nothing timeless in himself. For whither should he mount from the stream of time, and what could he win save useless suffering and a feeling of annihilation? One man balances the joys and sorrows of the past, seeking to focus upon a single image, under the lens of memory, the faint light that still glimmers out of the distance which he has traversed. Another reviews his achievements; it pleases him to recall his arduous struggle against the world and fate; and happy that matters have not turned out worse, he notes here

* "Even for a day," as in the case of the New Year's Day, around which the whole paragraph is oriented. See note on p. 12.

and there some monument to his effort, fashioned out of the stuff of a reality indifferent to his aims, though, of course, it falls far short of his intentions. Still a third takes stock of his learning, and struts with pride because of his much increased and well-appointed store of knowledge, delighted in his power to contain it all. What puerile attempts of an idle conceit are these! The first no longer thinks of the cares which his imagination raised for him, and which his memory blushes to preserve; the second turns his back upon the world and fate, refusing altogether to acknowledge the support they gave him; the third does not take into account the old knowledge that was crowded out by the new, the thoughts that thinking excluded, and the impressions that were sacrificed to learning. Thus the reckoning is never right. And if it were, how deeply pained I am to think that men can imagine this to be self-contemplation, or call this knowledge of oneself! How miserably their much glorified business of self-examination ends! Imagination fixes on a faithful portrait of the past, projects it with lavish embellishments upon the empty canvass of the immediate future, and yet looks back with many a sigh toward the original. The ultimate gain of such introspection reduces itself to the idle hope of a better future, and the vain lament that bygone pleasures are no more, and that life's substance as it wanes from day to day gives warning that its bright flame will soon expire. With such idle wishes and vain complaints Time grievously brands her slaves who would escape; the best are like unto the worst for she will just as surely overtake the best eventually. Whoever sees and recognizes only the outward spectacle of life instead of the spiritual activity that secretly stirs his inmost being, who merely constructs a picture of life and its vicissitudes from impressions gathered far and near instead of facing his essential self, will always remain a slave of Time and Necessity. All his thoughts and feelings bear their stamp, are still in their possession, and he may never set foot within the sacred precincts of Freedom, even though he thinks he has attained self-consciousness. For in the image which he constructs of himself, this very self becomes something external, like all else, and everything in such an image is determined by external circumstances. What he sees in it, the thoughts and feelings that it arouses, depend alike on the content of the moment and on his particular condition of life. If he has looked for nought but the gratification of animal sense, he will judge life rich or poor according to the number of agreeable moments it contains, and the immediate satisfaction which he takes in such a retrospect will depend on whether the greatest pleasures[11] came first or last. If he wanted to create and to enjoy beauty,[12] he will court the judgment passed upon him, and is dependent furthermore upon the conditions and materials that fate has provided for his work. In like dependence is he who sought to signalize his life with benefactions. They all must bow beneath the sceptre of Necessity, and bear the curse of transiency, which permits nothing to endure.

Their sense of life is like my mood when some artfully constructed harmony of many notes has struck my ear[13] but is now silent; the imagination plagues itself with a meagre echo, and the soul yearns for that which will not return. Life indeed is but a fleeting harmony rising from the contact of the temporal and the eternal, but man is a permanent creation,[14] an undying object of contemplation. Only[15] his innermost activity, wherein his true nature abides, is free,[16] and in contemplating it, I feel myself to be upon the holy ground of Freedom, far from every debasing limitation. I must fix my eyes upon my true self, if each moment is not to slip away as merely so much time, instead of being grasped as an element of Eternity, and transmuted into a higher and freer life.[17]

He alone enjoys freedom and eternity who knows[18] what man is and what the world is,[19] who has reached clarity in solving the great enigma of their differentiation and their interaction, a riddle in whose dark and ancient mazes thousands still are caught, and needs must follow servilely the most deceptive illusions, because their own light has failed them. What the multitude calls the world, I call man, and what they call man, I call the world.* To them the world is every primary,[20] and the spirit but a humble guest upon it, uncertain of his place and powers. To me the spirit is the first and only being,[21] for what I take to be the world, is the fairest creation of spirit, a mirror in which it is reflected. In awe and fear the multitude cower before the infinitely vast and ponderous masses of the material

* In this passage (pp. 16-17) Schleiermacher's revisions of 1810 are more fundamental than elsewhere. The change is from an extreme to a more modified "idealistic" idiom. Cf. pp. 128-130 and see notes on pp. 104-105.

world, amid which man appears so small and insignificant. To me all this is but the giant body common to Humanity, belonging to us even as an individual's body does to him, made possible through Humanity alone, to which it is given in order that the human spirit may master it and be revealed therein. The creative freedom of Humanity is exercized upon this body, to sense all its pulsations, to mold and transmute all its features into organs of human life, and to delineate all its parts with the spirit's regal presence.* Is there indeed a body without a spirit? Does not the body exist only because and insofar as the spirit requires it and is conscious thereof?[22] All those feelings that seem to be forced upon me by the material world are in reality my own free doing;[23] nothing is a mere effect of that world upon me, every real influence is exerted by me upon it;[24] that world is not, in fact, distinct from me, nor antithetic to me. For this very reason I do not choose to dignify it with the name of world, a great word implying omnipresence and omnipotence. The only reality that I deem worthy to be called a world is the eternal community of spiritual beings, their influence upon each other, their mutual development, the sublime harmony of freedom. This infinite totality of spiritual beings is the only reality that I recognize over against my finite and individual self. This reality alone I suffer to transform and shape the surface of my being; this heaven alone shall mold me. Here, and here only is the province of necessity. My activ-

* This description of the spirit's functions anticipates the distinction made in Schleiermacher's later systematic works between "organizing" and "symbolizing" activity. See pp. 146-147.

ity itself is free, not so my function in the world,[25] for that obeys eternal laws. Freedom finds its limit in another freedom, and whatever happens freely bears marks of limitation and community. Yes, holy Freedom, in all reality thou art first! It is thou that dwellest within me and in everyone. Outside us is Necessity, a chord determined by the harmonious clash of various inner liberties that thus reveal themselves. Within me I can behold nought but Freedom, necessity reigns not in my doing, but in the reflection thereof, in the perceptions I have[26] of the world which I help to create in holy[27] association with all other beings. To this realm of necessity belongs whatever I have produced in working on a common foundation with others; such productions are my share in the joint creation that expresses our inner thought. To necessity belong also the rising and falling tides of emotion, the train of images that passes before us, and everything that changes in our souls with time. Such images and feelings are a token that the spirit and the world have met in harmony, ever renewing the kiss of friendship between them in a different manner. The Dance of Hours thus proceeds, melodious and harmonious, according to a necessary rhythm. But Freedom plays the melody,[28] selects the key, and all the subtle modulations are her work. For these proceed from an inner determination and from the individual's unique disposition.

And so, Freedom, you are for me the soul and principle of all things. When I withdraw into myself to contemplate you, my eyes are lifted from the realm of time, and my vision free from every restriction of Necessity. Every oppressive feeling of bondage disappears, my spirit discovers its creative nature, the light of God begins to shine upon me, banishing far hence the mists in which enslaved humanity strays in error. The self revealed in my meditations is no longer a creature of fate or fortune; the hours of happiness I have deserved, the results achieved by my efforts, and whatever I have actually put into execution, all these are of the world; they are not myself. If my activity is designed to bring humanity into possession of its massive body, the material world, giving this body life and organic fitness, or by artful imitation fashioning it in the image of reason and mind,* the extent to which I find the earth already suited to my purpose, the ease with which its crude mass can be molded and brought under the control of spirit, is but[29] a sign of the dominion which Freedom has already exercised over it in the person of others. It indicates what still remains to be done, but furnishes no measure of what I do.[30] My view of my conduct and picture of my whole being is unchanged; I am no better or no worse in my own eyes, whether external circumstances are propitious or unfavorable to my activity.[31] I do not discover in myself the slave, for whom the world or ironbound necessity decides what he may become. And just as pain does not easily deprive a strong and healthy soul of control over the physical body, so too I sense my free dominion over the material world, regardless of whether the consequences be

* This passage (pp. 19-20) on the two possible aims of action is further elucidated by the theory of a fundamental dichotomy of human types explained on pp. 34-37 below.

pleasurable or painful. The inner life reveals itself alike in either case, and its creation is an act of spiritual freedom. If the purpose of my actions is to shape what is human in me,* giving it a particular form and definite characteristics, thus contributing to the world by my own self-development and offering to the community of free spiritual beings the unique expression of my own freedom, then I see no difference whether or not my efforts are at once combined with those of others and some objective result[32] immediately appears to greet me as part of the world-order. My efforts have not been vain, if only I myself acquire greater individuality and independence, for through such self-development I also contribute to the world, no matter how soon or late the actions of others combine with my own to produce some new, visible result. Unlike those who have not discovered the inner life, and who think to find themselves in particulars of the outward life, I am never depressed by self-contemplation, nor need I ever lament a broken will or a defeated purpose.

Having clearly differentiated between the inner and the outer, I know who I am, and I find myself only in the inner life,† in external things I see only the world. My spirit knows how to distinguish both, and does not fluctuate between the two, as is

* See note on p. 19.

† "I find myself only in the inner life." The point of this emphasis on self-analysis as the key to the meaning of life (cf. pp. 118-119) lies in Schleiermacher's repudiation of all attempts to find that meaning in some law, principle, or power outside of man's own purposes. In his earliest philosophical essays he criticizes Kant's theology and his conception of the categorical imperative from this standpoint. See pp. xxxii, 117, and *Schiele*, pp. 97-98.

common, in unenlightened confusion. Hence I also know where Freedom is to be sought and the sacred sense of its presence, that ever refuses to bless him whose vision rests solely upon the outward life and work of man. However deeply such a one may involve himself in endless mazes of speculation, turning the problem over and over, and however effective he may be in action, the conception of Freedom is beyond the reach of his thought. He follows not only the actual indications of necessity, but in slavish and superstitious submission to his false philosophy he must look for them and believe them to be present, even where he does not see them. Freedom seems to him nothing but an illusion, spread like a veil over a hidden and uncomprehended necessity.[33] Moreover, such an empiricist, whose action and whose thought look outward, sees everything as finite and particular. He cannot imagine himself as other than a sum of fleeting appearances, each of which supplants and cancels the other, so that it is impossible to conceive them as a whole. A complete picture of his being thus eludes him in a thousand contradictions. Indeed, in the realm of outward behavior particulars are often contradictory; action destroys passivity, thought supplants sensation, and contemplation forces the will to be at rest. But within the spirit all is one, each action is but supplementary to another, in each the other also is preserved.* Thus self-contemplation lifts me far above the finite, which may be seen entire as a determined series with definite limits. No action transpires within me, that I can truly regard as iso-

* Cf. pp. 71-72.

lated, and none of which I could say that it constitutes a whole by itself. Each of my acts reveals the whole of my being,[34] undivided, each of its manifestations goes with the rest; there are no limits at which introspection can halt, it must ever remain unfinished, if it is to remain true to life. Nor can I divine my own being in its entirety without contemplating Humanity, and determining my rank and place in its domain. And who can think of Humanity without being lost in thought of the pure spirit's infinite realm and nature?[35]*

It is this higher order of self-contemplation, and this alone that makes me capable of meeting the sublime summons that man live not only as a mortal in the realm of time, but also as immortal in the domain of eternity, that his life be not only earthly but also divine. The stream of time bears with it in its course my mortal deeds; ideas and feelings change, I can not hold fast a single one. The scene of life, as I picture it, hurries by; upon the next inevitable wave the stream will carry me on toward something new. But as often as I turn my gaze inward upon my inmost self, I am at once within the domain of eternity. I behold the spirit's action,[36] which no world can change, and no time can destroy, but which itself creates both world and time.† Nor do I require the challenge of that spe-

---

* This is one of several passages in the *Soliloquies*, suggesting that contemplation of the individual self, which yields the guiding principle of ethics, leads naturally into meditation upon universal being, the essence of religion. Cf. pp. 24, 140. I have tried to explain Schleiermacher's conception of the relation between individual and universe, ethics and religion on pp. xlix, 127, of the Introduction and Appendix.

† Cf. *On Religion*, pp. 70ff.

cial hour, in which one year gives way to another, to arouse me to this appreciation of the eternal, and to open the eyes of the spirit, closed perhaps[37] in slumber though the heart beats and the limbs are active. Who once has tasted it will want to lead the divine life continually; every act should be accompanied by an insight into spiritual mysteries, and in every moment man can dwell beyond the moment, in the higher world.

Of course, wise-men say:* to live is one thing, and to lose oneself in the ultimate sources and highest reaches of thought[38] is another. Content yourself modestly with one of them, for while the passage of time keeps you busy with the affairs of the world, you can not also contemplate the inmost depths of your being without distraction. Artists say that, when you are creating a picture or composing a poem, the mind must lose itself completely in its work, and must not reflect upon its own behavior. Nevertheless, dare to try, my soul, in spite of these reasonable warnings! Press forward toward your own goal, which may be different from that of artists and sages.† Man can do more than he supposes; yet even when he strives toward the highest, he can but achieve in part. If a sage's thought, even in its most intimate[39] and profound reaches, can be an external force of influence and guidance in the world, then why should not an outward act, of whatever nature, at the same time imply its own inward consideration?[40] If the divine source of all art and

* "Wise-men." This, too, is probably a thrust at Fichte, because of his contention that a certain antithesis ultimately remains between "life" and "philosophy." (*Schiele*, p. 99.)
† Cf. pp. 34-37.

poetry is spiritual introspection, and if the spirit finds within its own being all that it can express in its immortal creations, why should not every creative act of artist or poet, being but the expression of what is within him involve self-contemplation? Divide not your being, my soul, it is a permament whole that cannot forego its activity nor the knowledge thereof without self-destruction!* Let your influence be everywhere felt, and accomplish all that you can; follow the lead of your natural limitations and cultivate every means of spiritual association; bring out what is individual in you, and place the impress of your spirit on all that is about you; collaborate in the consecrated tasks of mankind, attracting to yourself such spirits as are congenial. But throughout all be ever mindful of your inner self, know what you are about, and in what character you are acting.[41] The idea, by which men imagine they have intellectually grasped the Deity, a thing they never can do,† has at least the truth of a poetic symbol of what humanity should be. The spirit sustains its world by the mere fact of its being, and the eternal, unchanging activity which produces its diverse acts issues from its own free will.‡ Itself unmoved, it contemplates its own activity, ever new and ever yet the same; this contemplation is immortality and eternal life, for therein the spirit requires nothing but itself,[42] and contemplation never lacks its object, nor does the object

* Cf. pp. 28.

†See p. 137, 140, in re Schleiermacher's opinion that the intellect can not know God.

‡ Cf. this passage with the description Schleiermacher gives of the God-idea in his systematic philosophical works. See below pp. 137, 140, 163.

lack the contemplating mind. In such terms men have also tried to imagine immortality, but all too content with the earthly life they aspire to it only after death.* Their mythology is more profound than they. In truth, to the sensuous mind an inner process can seem but the shadow of an outward act, and in such a realm of shadows men have placed the soul forever, lamenting[43] that the grey existence there below affords them but a meagre suggestion of their present life. But this spiritual life, which scant imagination exiles into subterranean darkness, is truly of Olympian clarity, and the realm of shadows may serve me here on earth as archetype of reality. God is thought to be outside the world of time, and after death man is to be freed forever from temporal limitations in order to behold and praise the Deity. But even now the spirit spans the world of time, Eternity is in the sight thereof, and the celestial rapture of immortal choirs. Wherefore begin at once your life eternal in the constant contemplation of your own true being. Be not troubled for the future, nor weep for things which pass, but take heed lest you lose yourself, and weep if you are swept along in the stream of time, without carrying heaven within you.

* Cf. this whole passage with the often-quoted section in the "Speeches" (*Reden*, p. 10, ed. by R. Otto) where Schleiermacher says: "Religion remained with me when God and immortality vanished before my doubts." See also pp. xv-xviii, above for the biographical background of these ideas.

II

SOUNDINGS

MANKIND is shy of self-analysis, and many people tremble slavishly when they can no longer dodge the question of what they have done, what they have become, and who they really are. The thing frightens them; they know not what will come of it. It seems to them easier for a man to judge another person than himself, and after strict self-scrutiny they rather claim the grace of modesty in giving themselves the benefit of the doubt. And yet it is only wilfullness that hides a person from himself; his judgment cannot err provided he really faces himself. But it is just this which people neither can nor want to do. The spell of life and of the world is upon them, and resolved not to turn from that spectacle, all that they discover of themselves is but a vague and delusive reflection.* To be sure, I can judge another person only by his acts, for I never look upon his inner disposition. I can never know at first hand what his purpose actually was; I simply compare his deeds with one another, and from these I make a precarious inference as to his aims and the spirit which moved him. But oh the shame of it, that anyone should see himself only as one stranger sees another! that anyone should remain ignorant of his inner life and even plume

* Cf. pp. 13-16.

himself on his supposed shrewdness, if he succeeds in grasping the last link of a chain of resolutions that issued in overt action, together with the feeling that attended it and the idea that immediately preceded it! How can such a one ever know either himself or others? What is to guide him in conjecturing inner realities from external facts, if he does not base his judgment on a crucial experience of something immediately certain?[1] The inevitable[2] presentiment of error makes him afraid, the overshadowing suspicion that he is culpable in his error oppresses his heart, and his thoughts vacillate in terror of that little portion of self-consciousness which men still carry with them, generally degraded to the rôle of a harsh disciplinarian, whose voice they needs must often hear unwillingly.*

In truth, men have good cause for anxiety, lest in honestly probing the inner motives of their lives, they fail to recognize what is truly human[3] there, and see the conscience, which is consciousness of true humanity, sadly mutilated. For whoever has not scrutinized his previous conduct can give no security that in the future he will remember that he is a human being, or prove himself worthy of the name. If he has once broken the thread of self-consciousness, if he has but once abandoned himself to those feelings and impressions that he shares with brutes,[4] how can he know whether he has not

* Three views of conscience are contrasted in what follows: (1) the popular view of conscience as "a little portion of self-consciousness degraded to the role of a disciplinarian." (2) Fichte's view: conscience is "consciousness of true humanity," the universal self in the individual self, and (3) Schleiermacher's own view: conscience is consciousness of one's unique place in true humanity. Cf. reference in *Schiele*, p. 99.

fallen into sheer brutality? To behold humanity within oneself, and never to lose sight of the vision when once found, is the only certain means of never straying from its sacred precincts.[5] This vision is the intimate and necessary tie between conduct and the perception of truth,* a connection mysterious and unintelligible only to fools and men of dull sensibility.† A truly human way of acting produces a clear consciousness of what is essentially human, and this in turn permits of no other behavior than such as is worthy of humanity. He who can never lift himself to this clear insight is ever the sport of vague instinctive premonitions; in vain you will undertake to educate and train him. For all his ingenuity and for all his bold resolution to force his way back into the circle of humanity,[6] the sacred portals will not open. He remains outside on profane ground, and he will not escape the pursuit of the offended god-head, nor the shameful feeling that he is an exile from his true fatherland. It is sheer folly and vain trifling to make experiments or to lay down rules in the realm of freedom. To be a man calls for a single free resolve; he who has taken that resolve will always remain one; he who ceases to be one has never taken it.‡

With proud joy I still recall the time, when I dis-

* I. E., knowledge of the ideal self is the necessary tie between theory and practice. For other statements of Schleiermacher's as to their connection see pp. 24, 42.

† "Fools . . . dull sensibility." Cf. Luke, XXIV, 25, "the foolish and slow of heart."

‡ Cf. pp. 73-74. In the autobiographical passages which follow Schleiermacher uses the language of religious awakening, particularly the language of German pietism, to describe his development. The Introduction (pp. xvii, xxxiii-xxxv) should be consulted for some of the facts referred to.

covered humanity[7] and knew that henceforth I should never lose it. The sublime revelation came from within; it was not produced by any code of ethics or system of philosophy. My long quest which neither this nor that would satisfy was crowned in one moment of insight; freedom dissolved my dark doubts by a single act. I can affirm that since then I have never forsaken my true self. I no longer know the thing that men call conscience; no qualm now reproves me, and I need none to warn me. Neither do I strive since then to acquire this or that particular virtue, nor am I especially elated by some particular act, as are those whose fleeting existence is only now and then visited by a dubious gleam of innate reason. In quiet tranquillity, in utter simplicity I preserve within me an uninterrupted consciousness of humanity's entire essence.* With pleasure and confidence I often survey my behavior in all its bearings, being assured that I shall find nothing which humanity[8] must needs repudiate. If this were all that I exacted of myself, I might long since have found inward peace, and awaited the end of my existence with perfect composure! For the certainty I have attained is unshakeable, and I should deem it a culpable piece of cowardice, such as is foreign to my nature, were I to look to a long life for fuller confirmation of my inner conviction, fearing that after all, something might yet happen that could plunge me from the height of reason into an abyss of sheer brutishness.[9] And yet, I too am still troubled with doubts. For

* Seven years earlier in an essay on *The Value of Life* (see Appendix, pp. 118-119, and *Schiele*, pp. 166-198), Schleiermacher had been less confident and self-possessed.

when I had reached my first goal, another and a higher appeared before me, and since it appears sometimes clearly and then again dimly, self-scrutiny does not always tell me by what path I can approach it, or where I stand with reference to it. On these points my judgment wavers. But it is confirmed and gains conviction the more often I return to examine myself. And however far I were from certainty, I should still search in silence and without complaint, for stronger than my doubt is my great joy in having found out what I should seek, and in escaping from the great illusion which deceives many of the best throughout their lives,* and keeps them from soaring to the true summits of humanity.[10] For a long time I too was content with the discovery of a universal reason; I worshipped the one essential being as the highest, and so believed that there is but a single right way of acting in every situation, that the conduct of all men should be alike, each differing from the other only by reason of his[11] place and station in the world. I thought humanity revealed itself as varied only in the manifold diversity of outward acts, that man[12] himself, the individual, was not a being uniquely fashioned, but of one substance and everywhere the same.[13]

Thus is it ever with mankind![14] When, turning with discontent from the unworthy particularity of a sensuous animal life, man wins a realization of humanity in its universal aspects and submits himself to duty,† he is not straightway capable of

* He means, for instance, Kant and Fichte, and those who think with them that the universal reason is the highest.
† Kantian ethics. See note on p. 27, and cf. pp. xxxviii-xl.

rising to[15] the still higher level of individuality in growth and in morality, nor to perceive and understand the unique nature which freedom chooses for herself[16] in each individual.* Most men rise but midway, expressing in fact[17] only a raw elementary humanity, simply because they have not grasped the thought of their own higher being. As for me, it is this which has taken hold of me. The sense of freedom alone did not content me; it gave no meaning to my personality, nor to the peculiar unity of the transient stream of consciousness flowing within me, which urged me to seek something of higher ethical value of which it was the sign. I was not satisfied to view humanity in rough unshapen masses, inwardly altogether alike, and taking transient shape externally only by reason of mutual contact and friction.[18]

Thus there dawned upon me what is now my highest intuition. I saw clearly that each man is meant to represent humanity in his own way, combining its elements uniquely, so that it may reveal itself in every mode, and all[19] that can issue from its womb be made actual in the fullness of unending space and time.† This thought alone[20] has uplifted me, and set me apart from everything common and untransformed in my surroundings; it has made of me an elect creation of the godhead, rejoicing in a unique form and character. The act of freedom,‡ which accompanied this inspiration has assembled

* This "choice of a nature by freedom" is better described in B and C, and also below on page 31-32. BC on p. 106.

† Cf. *On Religion*, pp. 72ff.

‡ "The act of freedom": cf. above p. 28, and note on same page.

and integrated the elements of human nature to make a unique existence. Had I from that time on surveyed the unique in my activity as constantly as I have always looked upon the universally human aspect of it, had I taken conscious possession of every action and limitation which were the consequence of that initial act of free determination, and had I given undisturbed attention to the further development of my unique nature and to each expression thereof, I could have no further doubt which province of humanity is mine, nor where to seek for the common principle which governs both the extension and the limitations of my growth. I should then have measured accurately the whole content of my being, ascertained my boundaries at every point, and should have known prophetically what I might yet be and might become. But tardily and only with great difficulty, does man reach the full knowledge of his individuality. He does not always dare to look toward it as his ideal, but prefers to turn his eyes upon the good which he possesses in common with humanity in general. Clinging to this common good with love and gratitude, he often doubts whether he should again separate his individual self from it.[21] Confusing the sensuous with the spiritual, he fears lest he sink back into that culpably limited kind of external personality which preceded his new insight, and not until late does he learn to value and rightly use his highest privilege. Thus interrupted the consciousness of individuality must for a long time remain vacillating. The most characteristic efforts of one's nature often go unobserved, and when its limitations are most clearly apparent, the eye too readily skims over them, and fastens on something universal, where it might have found the unique by reason of its very limitations. However, I may be content with the way my will has conquered inertia, and practice trained my eye so that little now escapes it. Whenever I now act in keeping with my own spirit and disposition, my imagination gives me the clearest proof that I do so by free, individual choice, in suggesting to me a thousand other ways of acting in a different spirit, yet all also consistent with the universal laws of humanity. I project myself into a thousand different likenesses in order to behold my own more clearly.

But since the picture of my individuality does not yet present itself to me complete in all its features, and is not yet certified by an unbroken continuity of clear self-consciousness,* I am not yet able to maintain an attitude of unvarying, tranquil assurance in my self-contemplation. Often I must deliberately review all my efforts and actions, recall my history; nor must I disregard the opinions of my friends, whom I have gladly suffered to look into the depths of my inner life, if they differ from my own judgment. It is true that in my own eyes I still seem to be the same man I was when my higher life began, only more firm and more defined. And, indeed, how should a man, having once attained an independent and unique character, suddenly take on another nature in the very midst of

* Cf. this "still broken continuity of self-consciousness" with the "unbroken consciousness of universal humanity" mentioned above, p. 29. For the autobiographical significance, consult pp. xxxi-xli (Introduction) and of course *Dilthey*.

his development and cultivation? How could he appropriate another side of human nature without having brought the first to its perfection? How could he wish to do it? And how could it occur without his knowing it?[22] Either I have never understood myself, or I am still the person I believed myself to be, and every seeming contradiction, when solved by self-scrutiny, must reveal more clearly where and how the various strands of my own being are concealed[23] and intertwined.

I am convinced that there is a two-fold vocation of men on earth, and it still seems to me to mark a great dichotomy in human nature.[24] To develop one's inner humanity into distinctness, expressing it in manifold acts, is one thing, to project it into works of art which clearly convey to everyone who looks at them whatever their creator intended to show, is a totally different thing.* He who is still on the lowest level, in the vestibule of uniqueness, fearing to limit himself by further decision, may seek to combine both courses with the result that he will not go far in either direction. Whosoever would really attain the one must let the other go. Not till the very end of life's development is there a bridge from one to the other, and it is open only to perfection such as man seldom reaches.†
How could I ever be in doubt as to my own choice? I have so emphatically eschewed everything that

* Cf. pp. 19-20.

† At one point in his diary (see *Dilthey*; Appendix, p. 113). Schleiermacher says only God reaches it. (Cf. *Schiele*, p. 102.)

makes the artist;* I have so eagerly made my own whatever serves the culture of the self, whatever hastens and confirms its development. The artist is on the alert for whatsoever may serve as sign and symbol of humanity; he ransacks the treasury of language, and builds a world of music from a chaos of sound; he searches for a hidden meaning and a harmony in nature's lovely play of colors. In any work which he conceives he first investigates the effect of every part, and searches out the law and structure of the whole, rejoicing more in the artistic vessel than in its costly content. Thereafter, ideas rise in his mind and shape themselves into new artistic creations; secretly he cherishes them in his soul; they grow in hidden silence. His productive energy knows no rest; he passes from project to execution and from execution to project; through constant practice his skill improves steadily; his riper judgment gives rein and check unto his fancy. This is the way that a creative nature advances toward the goal of perfection.

But all this I learned by observation,[25]† for it is alien to my thought.[26] The humanity represented in a work of art stands out much more luminous and clear to me than the artist's artistry. The lat-

* I have tried to explain the motivation and significance of the ensuing passage (pp. 34-41) in the Introduction, pp. xxxviii-xli. Schleiermacher keenly felt the lack of creative, artistic power for two reasons especially: (1) because his closest friends in the "romantic group," Schlegel et al, had something of it and exalted it as the supreme form of spirituality, and (2) because he himself believed that art was the true language of religion, which was for him the highest. (See *Dilthey*, p. 289, N. E. 323. See also *On Religion*, p. 139.)

† "By observation" of his artist friends in the romantic circle. See pp. xxxviii-xl.

ter I get only with effort and later study, and then only enough to understand it a little. I like[27] nature's free artistry just as it is; her lovely and meaningful signs awaken impressions and ideas in me without the impulse to force them into a more constricted form of my own creation. I do not insist upon a perfect treatment of the material in which my thought is expressed.[28] And therefore I refrain from acquiring the utmost skill by practice, and when I have once put forth in action what is within me, I care not whether the act be often renewed in fairer and clearer fashion. Leisure is my dear divinity;* by her favor man learns[29] to understand and to determine himself. It is in leisure that ideas ripen unto power which easily governs all when the world calls for action. It follows also that I can not work in isolation like the artist; in solitude the juices of my spirit are dried up, my thought stands still. I must go forth and enter into manifold association with others in order[30] to behold what types of humanity there are, which of them are still alien to me, which I can assimilate, ever determining[31] my own being more decidedly by mutual give and take. My unquenched thirst for ever continuing self-development does not permit me to give the expression of my inner life an external finish. I simply launch my word and deed upon the world, nothing mindful whether observers have the sense to penetrate a crude exterior and happily to find the inner meaning, the unique spirit even in its less perfect manifestations. I have

* "Leisure" in contrast to the artist's diligence just described. Cf. *Letters*, v. 1, pp. 170ff., and 268.

neither time nor inclination for this; I must be up and doing, moving on beyond my last position, bringing my own being to its completion, if[32] that be possible in this short life, through new activity and thought. I hate even to try the same thing twice, so little is there of the artist in me. Hence, everything I do, I like to do in the company of others; even while engaged in meditation, in contemplation, or in the assimilation of anything new, I need the presence of some loved one, so that the inner event may immediately be communicated, and I may forthwith make my account with the world through the sweet and easy mediation of friendship. So was it, so is it now, and I am still so distant from my goal that I should be mistaken in thinking it will ever be otherwise.[33] Surely I am right, whatever friends may say, in excluding myself from the territory sacred to artists. Gladly do I renounce everything with which they have credited me, provided only that I find myself less imperfect than they imagine in the field where I have taken up my stand.

Reveal thyself to me once more, oh fair vision of that wide realm of humanity, where dwell all those who seek only to realize themselves,[34] and to express themselves in manifold activities, without creating any permanent monument of their labor! Reveal thyself once more, and let me see whether a place of my own belongs to me in thy realm. Let me behold whether there is coherence within me, or whether some intrinsic contrarieties prevent the image of myself from closing into unity, so that my own being like some miscarried sketch instead of attaining its perfection dissolves into emptiness and unreality. O no, I need not fear, no sad presentiment of failure possesses my soul! I recognize that all within me articulates to form a genuine whole, no foreign element in my nature oppresses me, no organ is missing, nor any member eligible for my unique life.* Whoever would make of himself a distinctive individual must be keen to perceive what he is not. For here, too, even in the realm of morality at its highest, that intimate connection between action and the perception of truth obtains.† Only if man is conscious of his individuality in his present conduct can he be sure of not violating it in his next act,[35] and only if he requires himself constantly to survey the whole of humanity, opposing his own expression of it to every other possible one, can he maintain the consciousness of his unique selfhood. For contrast is indispensable to set the individuality in relief. The highest[36] condition of individual perfection in a limited field is a general sensitiveness.‡ And how can this subsist apart from love? Without love, the very first attempt at self-formation would prove shattering because of the frightful dis-

* "No sad presentiment, . . . I recognize . . . no organ is missing," i. e., feeling, knowing, and acting testify to my being a complete whole. Cf. pp. 118, 141-142, for Schleiermacher's treatment of this traditional three-fold division of the soul's activity.

† That "intimate connection" which obtains also in the realm of elementary morality, the same for all. See above p. 28 and note on the same page.

‡ The ensuing passage (pp. 38-43) on "sensitiveness" and "love" as the cardinal conditions of moral perfection is central. "Sensitiveness" is receptive, the quality which at its deepest Schleiermacher describes in the "Speeches" (*On Religion*) as "sense and taste for the infinite," the capacity for revelations. See pp. xlviiiff. Love is predominantly active and out-going, is the basis of true association, and must balance sensitiveness. See pp. xlviii-xlix, 87-88.

proportion between giving and receiving; the mind would be forced to some extreme one-sidedness, and he who made the attempt in this fashion would either be wholly broken or else sink to the vulgar level. Love, thou force of gravitation in the spiritual world, no individual life and no development is possible without thee!* Without thee all things would flow together in a crude and homogeneous mass! Those who do not care to rise above this condition have little need of you; law and duty suffice for them, uniformity in conduct, and justice.† For such as these the sacred sense of love would be a useless treasure, and this is why they let the little of it that they have grow wild, uncultivated. Not recognizing its sacredness, they cast it carelessly into the common pool of human goods, that should be governed according to a universal law. But for us, O love, thou art the alpha and omega.‡ No development without love, and without individual development no perfection in love; each supplements the other, both increase indivisibly. I feel both of the highest conditions of morality united within me! I have made both sensitiveness and love my own, and both are ever waxing, a sure sign that my life is fresh and healthy, and that my individuality will develop more. Is there anything that lies beyond the range of my sensitiveness? Those[37] who would have every one become a virtuoso and expert in some field of knowledge are wont to complain of me, that I will not suffer myself to be

* Cf. the ensuing passage with the parallel one on love in the "Speeches," *On Religion*, pp. 72-84.
† Another touch in the polemic against Kant and Fichte. Cf. pp. 30ff.
‡ "Us," i. e., the "romanticists."

pinned down, that it is useless to hope I should ever seriously devote myself to some one thing. They say that when I have succeeded in gaining a certain view of things, my mind hastens on in its usual, restless, superficial fashion to other objects. Would that they leave me in peace, understanding that this is my destiny, that I must not devote myself to science,[38] because I am set upon the development of myself! Would that they allowed me to keep my mind open toward all their busy endeavors, considering what I fashion within me as I contemplate their activities worth while their trouble! And yet their very complaints witness in my behalf. For there are others who are likewise dissatisfied with me, but for the opposite reason. These while unlike me in nature are nevertheless like me seeking to penetrate into the very center of humanity. They say my appreciation is fundamentally limited, that I can pass by indifferent to many sacred things, and spoil my deep innocent insight by vain contentiousness.* Yes, I do still pass by much, but not with indifference. I dispute, but only to maintain my vision clear and open. Whenever I feel conscious of some expression of humanity that I have not mastered, my first concern is to dispute, not indeed whether it exists, but whether it is of such a nature, and only such, as is shown me by him in whom I first encounter it. My late awakened spirit, remembering how long it bore an alien yoke,† fears ever

* Schiele says: "Schleiermacher here defends himself against charges which Fr. Schlegel brought against him in his *Lucinde* in the person of Antonio. *Lucinde*, pp. 272ff. *Dilthey*, p. 459," N. E. 503. (*Schiele*, p. 104.)

† Refers to his early education in the Moravian seminary. See Introduction, pp. xv-xviii.

lest it be subjected again to the domination of some alien opinion, and whenever a strange object discloses a new aspect of life, my first step is to rise in arms against it, in order to fight for freedom and not to fall back at every new experience into the slavery in which my education began.[39] As soon, however, as I have won my distinctive point of view, the time for strife is over, and I gladly suffer each other view to take its place beside my own; my mind in peace completes the work of penetrating and interpreting each other standpoint.

Thus it is, that what may often seem a limitation of my sensitiveness is really but the first stir of appreciation within me. To be sure, I have very often had to assert myself positively, during this beautiful time of my life,* when I came into contact with so much that was new to me, when so much became broad daylight to me which I had but darkly sensed before, and for which I had no preparation! Often I was obliged to appear antagonistic to those who were a source of new insight for me. Unperturbed I have suffered their misapprehension, trusting that they would understand, as soon as they had entered more deeply into my nature. Even my friends have frequently misunderstood me in this way, especially when I passed by unsympathetically, though not with enmity, things which ardently appealed to them and excited their zeal. The mind cannot apprehend all things at once: it is useless for it to try to finish its task by a single effort; its process must be continuous in two directions,

* I. E., during his first residence in Berlin when he met Schlegel and his other associates. See Introduction, pp. xxxviiff. and, of course, *Dilthey*, pp. 182-296; N. E., 218-331.

and each man has his own way of combining both in order to make up the whole.* For me it is impossible, when anything new presents itself, to penetrate at once into its core with burning intensity and get to know it perfectly. Such an attempt would ill beseem that equanimity which is the keynote of my being's harmony. To seize upon some such particular would upset the balance of my life, and while I became absorbed in that one thing I should lose contact with the rest, without even making the first truly my own. I must first store up every new acquisition in my mind, and then let the usual forces of my life play upon it and about it, so that the new shall be mingled with the old, and come into touch with everything that I already harbor within me. Only by such activity as this do I succeed in preparing the way for a deeper and more intimate perception; contemplation and practice must often alternate before I am satisfied that I have fathomed anything. Thus and thus alone can I go about my business, if I am not to violate my inner being, for in me self-development and activity turned beyond the self must balance at every moment. Therefore my progress is slow, and I shall have to live long before I have embraced all things equally, but whatever I do embrace will bear my impress.† Whatever part of humanity's infinite realm I have apprehended will

* The direction of predominantly receptive "sensitiveness" and that of predominantly active "love." Cf. Appendix, pp. 146ff., for Schleiermacher's treatment of these two in his later systematic works as the "symbolizing" and "organizing" functions of spirit respectively. Cf. also with other passages of the *Soliloquies*, especially pp. 19-20.

† "Impress," as result of the "symbolizing" function of spirit. See pp. 17, 64.

be in equal measure uniquely transformed and taken up into my being.[40]

Oh how much richer my life has become! What sweet awareness of inner[41] worth, what enhanced assurance of individuality rewards me when I survey the profit of so many happy and prosperous days! My silent effort, though it appear like mere idleness from without,* was not in vain; it has well served my inward task of self-development. Mistaken outward activity ill-suited to my nature would not have carried this so far, and restricting the range of my appreciation would have impeded it still more.† Alas that a man's inner character should be so misjudged, even by those who might understand and who deserve to recognize it everywhere! Alas that so many, even of these, confuse outward behavior and inner activity, deeming it possible to construe the latter like the former from fragmentary appearances, and suspecting contradiction where everything fits to perfection! Is then my real character so hard to recognize? Am I ever to forego my heart's dearest desire to show myself as I am to all my worthy fellow men? For even now, as I look deeply into my nature, I am confirmed anew in the conviction that this is the strongest motive in my being. This is the truth, no matter how often I am told that I am shut up in myself, and that I often coldly repel the hallowed advances of love and friendship. To be sure, I never deem

* It touched the romanticists closely to distinguish between good and bad idleness. Cf. Schlegel's *Lucinde*, and a sermon of Schleiermacher's on the subject, *Werke*, II, v. 1, pp. 109ff.
† I. E., neither art nor science was his proper vocation. Cf. above pp. 34-41.

it necessary to talk of what I have done or what has happened to me. In my view, the worldly part of me is too insignificant that I should weary by dwelling on it, those whom I would gladly wish to have know me inwardly. Nor do I care to speak of that which is still dark and unformed within me lacking that clarity which makes it mine. How should I offer to my friend what does not yet belong to me? Why thereby hide from him what I already am? How could I hope to communicate, without raising up misunderstanding, that which I do not yet understand myself? Such an attitude on my part does not argue reticence and lack of love. Rather is it the evidence of a holy reverence without which there is no real love; it is the instinct of delicacy that would not profane the highest, nor needlessly obscure it. As soon as I have genuinely appropriated anything new in respect to culture and individuality, from whatever source, do I not run to my friend in word and deed to let him know of it, that he may share my joy, and himself profit as he perceives understandingly my inner growth? My friend I cherish as my own self; whatever I come to recognize as my own, I place straightway at his disposal. It is true I sometimes take less interest than do those who call themselves his friends in what he does and in that which happens to him. His outward behavior neither affects nor concerns me, if I already understand the inner being whence it flows, and know that it must of necessity be thus, because my friend is such as he is. This outward side of him neither feeds nor excites my love for him, has no relation to it.[42] It belongs to the world and with all its consequences must conform to the laws of necessity.* But whatever the consequences, whatever happens to my friend, he will surely know how to act with a freedom worthy of himself. And nothing else concerns me. I contemplate his fate with calmness even as I do my own. Who will regard this as cold indifference? A clear appreciation of the contrast between world and man is the ground on which all self-respect and sense of freedom rest. Should I grant this less unto my friend than unto myself?

This is the very thing of which I chiefly boast, that my love and friendship always have so high a source,[43] that they have never been blended with any vulgar sentiment, have never been the offspring of habit or tender feeling, but ever an act of purest freedom, orientated towards the individuality of other human beings. I have ever kept the more common sentiment at a distance from myself. A benefit has never bribed me into friendship, nor has beauty stolen my love. Pity has never so enmeshed my judgment that it ascribed a merit to misfortune and represented suffering human beings as otherwise and better than they are.[44] And so a place was cleared in my soul for genuine love and friendship, and my longing to fill this space with ever larger and more manifold content never abates. Wherever I notice an aptitude for individuality, inasmuch as love and sensitiveness, its highest guarantees, are present, there I also find an object for my love. I would have my love embrace every unique self, from the unsophisticated youth, in whom freedom

*Cf. pp. 18ff.

is but beginning to germinate, to the ripest and most finished type of man. Whenever I see such a one, I give him the salutation of the love within me, even if our brief meeting and parting permit no more than this gesture of spiritual greeting. Neither do I measure my friendship for anyone by any worldly standard of external appearances. My vision soars beyond the worldly and temporal, seeking inner greatness. Whether he to whom I would be a friend is already sensitive to much or little, whether he is or is not far advanced in his development, whether he has many achievements to his credit or not, all these things may not determine my attitude toward him, and whatever is missing in this respect I can easily dispense with. His unique being and its relation to humanity is the object of my quest. I love him in the measure that I find and understand this individuality, but I can give him proof thereof only in proportion to his understanding of my own true self. Alas, often did this love of mine return to me uncomprehended, the language of the heart was not heard, as if I had remained dumb, and those to whom I would have shown my love actually believed I had.

Men often travel in neighboring ways, and yet are not near each other. The one divines a friendly presence and is inclined toward friendly greeting. He calls but calls in vain; the other does not hear him. Frequently opposites approach each other,[45] and henceforth there is to be no more separation. But their encounter is for a moment only, and movements in opposite directions sweep them from each other's ken, neither knowing whither the other has disappeared. This has often befallen me in my longing for love. Would it not be shameful, if I had not at last been disciplined, if my all too easy optimism had not fled, and experienced wisdom taken its place? "Here is one who will understand you in part, there another who will understand a different side of you; a certain kind of love is possible toward the one, but beware how you offer it to the other." Thus am I often vainly warned to be discreet. For the urge of my heart leaves little room for prudence;* much less can I presume to assign limits to other men, and to say how far they should respond to me and to my love. I always take too much for granted, I always try again, and am forthwith punished for my avarice by losing what I had already gained. But no other fortune is possible for one who is engaged in forming himself, and that I suffer thus is the surest proof that I am so engaged. A person so occupied, uniquely combines in himself various elements of humanity.[46] He belongs to more than one world. How could he move in an orbit exactly parallel to that of another, who is also a distinctive individual, how continue in his neighborhood?† Like a comet the cultured individual traverses many systems and encircles many a sun.‡ Now he passes a certain star which sees him gladly, and seeks to know him; he on his part bends his course with friendly intent in that star's

* As to Schleiermacher's prudence, cf. pp. xxxiv, 89, 100-103.
† Explanation of apparent waywardness and fleeting attachments that the non-romanticist fails to understand. The meaning is clearer in B and C; see pp. 108.
‡ He belongs to "more than one world," . . . "traverses many systems," "many a sun." Cf. Schleiermacher's development of this theme in the fourth *Soliloquy*, pp. 76, 81-88 below.

direction. Then lo! he has moved away into far-off spaces, his very shape seems changed; there is a doubt whether he is still the same. But anon he returns in swift revolution and there takes place anew a passing interchange of love and friendship. But where find the fair ideal of complete and permanent union, of friendship perfect on both sides? Only where on both sides love and sensitiveness have increased in equal measure as it were beyond all measure. But then, in such a perfect love the individuals themselves are also made perfect.* The hour is at hand—ah! for all of us it strikes much sooner—to yield up finite existence, and to return out of the world to the bosom of the infinite.

---

* Cf. the fuller exposition of this idea at the end of the fourth *Soliloquy*, p. 87-88. Schleiermacher thought of the first *Soliloquy* as symmetrical with the third, the second with the fourth, both in respect to content and style. See *Schiele,* p. xxxiv.

III

THE WORLD

DREAR old age, they say, has the right to complain about the world; it may be pardoned for preferring to look back on better days when life was at the full. Joyous youth should smile upon life, ignoring defects, making the most of what is there, and trusting readily to the sweet deceits of hope. But the truth, a correct estimate of the world, is credited to him alone, who secure in the contentment of middle age, neither vainly grieves nor falsely hopes. Such contentment, however, is but folly's passage from hope in life to contempt for it; such wisdom but the hollow echo of footsteps reluctantly moving on from youth to age; such satisfaction is a stupid turn of make-believe courtesy on the part of one who would escape outright impeachment of a world, in which his stay is bound to be soon cut short, and who would no less avoid impeaching his own judgment; such praise of middle-life is vanity ashamed of its mistakes, it is a forgetting of recent desires, it is the complacency which contents itself with poverty rather than submit to toil. I did not flatter myself when I was young, and therefore, I do not flatter the world now, nor at any time. It cannot disappoint one who expects nothing, nor will he offend it in revenge. I have done little to make things what they are, and so I need not expect to find them better. Nothing disgusts me more than the vile praise which is lavished on the world from all sides, by those who wish to shine in the reflected light of their own handiwork. This perverse generation loves to talk of how it has improved the world, in order to plume itself and to be considered superior to its ancestors. Were perfected human nature already in blossom and diffusing its first sweet fragrance, were the seeds of self-culture for ever so many individuals already assured of their growth on the soil of a common civilization, if the breath of every life were already free and sacred, and if a pervasive love drew all humanity into miraculous relationships ever productive of new and marvelous fruit,—even then this generation could not outdo its glittering praise of mankind's present estate. To hear them discourse on the world of today, one would imagine the thundering voice of their mighty reason[1] had burst the chains of ignorance, that they had at last succeeded in setting up a perfect portrait of human nature, which formerly had been painted obscurely in colors of darkness so as to be scarcely recognizable,* but which now was marvelously illumined by light from above,[2] so that no sane vision could longer mistake the general outlines or even the individual traits; they speak as if the music of their wisdom had transformed raw, predatory self-seeking into the tamest house-pet and taught it the arts. Every least moment is supposed to have been full of progress. O how deeply I despise this generation, which

* The phrase "colors of darkness" no doubt characterizes the doctrine of human depravity which the Enlightenment attacked.

plumes itself more shamelessly than any previous one ever did, which can scarcely endure the belief in a still better future and reviles everyone who dedicates himself thereto, simply because the true goal of mankind, toward which the age has risked scarcely a single step, lies unknown to it in the dim distance!

Of course, if one is content to have man control the material world alone, tapping all its powers for his own service,[3] and conquering space so that it no longer cripples the strength of his spirit,[4] the mere nod of his will instantly and everywhere producing the action it intends, with all things under the dominion of ideas and the spirit's presence everywhere revealed; whoever is content to see crude matter vitalized and to have mankind find the joy of living in the consciousness of mastering its body,[5]*—let him, for whom this is the ultimate aim, join in the noisy praise of our times. For now as never before may man justly boast such mastery. However much remains undone, enough has been accomplished to make him feel lord of the earth, believing that nothing may be left unattempted in this, his own particular domain, and that the concept[6] of impossibility, ever narrowing, must finally vanish altogether. In respect to this purpose I feel that communion with mankind augments my own powers in every moment of my life. Each of us plies his own particular trade, completing the work of someone whom he never knew, or preparing the way for another who in turn will scarcely recognize

---

* "Its body" here means the whole material world. Cf. above pp. 16-17.

how much he owes to him. Thus the work[7] of humanity is promoted throughout the world; everyone feels the influence of others as part of his own life; by the ingenious mechanism of this community the slightest movement of each individual is conducted like an electric spark, through a long chain of a thousand living links, greatly amplifying its final effect; all are, as it were, members of a great organism, and whatever they may have done severally, is instantaneously consummated as its work. Probably this sense of life's enhancement by common effort is more vividly and more satisfyingly present in me than in those who are so loud in its praise. For I am not disturbed and disappointed by their gloomy supposition that the gains, which all helped to produce and to maintain are enjoyed so unequally. Lazy thinking and emptiness of mind can be but a loss to anyone, habit levies it, tax on us all, and whenever I compare a person's restrictions with his powers, I arrive at the same ratio, expressing in different ways an equal measure of life for all.* But even so I regard this whole sense of a common material progress to be of little value; it is not further gain in this direction that I desire for the world; it causes me mortal agony that this, an unholy waste of its holy powers, should be regarded as mankind's entire task. My demands are not so modest as to be content with the improvement of man's relation to external nature, even though this relation were already brought to the

* The thought here seems somewhat forced. The field to which a person's activity is restricted varies with the extent of his powers. Life demands much from him to whom it gives much, and the ratio between give and take is the same for all.

highest point of perfection![8] Is man then merely a creature of the senses, for whom a heightened feeling of vitality, of health and strength can be the highest good? Is the spirit satisfied to inhabit the body, extending and augmenting its powers in conscious mastery thereof? For this is the multitude's whole ambition, and upon such achievements they base their unmeasured pride. From caring for their own physical existence and well-being they have come to care for the similar well-being of all, but that is as far as they have risen in their consciousness of humanity. That is what virtue, justice, and love mean to them; that is the essence of their noisy triumph over base self-seeking; that is the end of all their wisdom, and such are the only links they are able to break in the chain of ignorance; everybody is to co-operate and every association is to be formed for an aim no higher than this. O what a perversion to think a man should devote his spiritual powers to secure for others what he himself spurns as inferior! How disfigured the mind which deems it a virtue to sacrifice the highest in such low idolatry!

Accept thy harsh lot, O my soul, to have seen the light only in such dark and wretched days. You can hope for naught from such a world to further your aspirations, it offers nothing for your inner development! You will necessarily find association with it a limitation, rather than an enhancement of your powers. All who know the higher ambitions experience this. Many a human heart thirsts for love; many a man is haunted by the image of an ideal companion[9] with whom close interchange of thought and feeling would prove mutually profitable and elevating,[10] but unless perchance he discovers such a friend within his own narrow circle, both he and that other consume their brief lives in a mutual longing.[11] The earth's resources and their location are described by thousands; I can learn in a moment where any material thing I need is to be found, and in the next I can possess it.[12] But no means exists for discovering such a personality, as is indispensable to the nurture of my inner life.[13] Society is not organized for such a purpose; to bring together those who need each other is no one's business. And even if he, whose heart seeks love everywhere in vain, should learn where dwelt his friend and his beloved, yet would he be restricted by his station in life, by the rank which he holds in that meagre thing we call society. Man clings to these restricting ties more tenaciously than stone or plant to mother earth. The piteous fate of the negro, torn from his loved ones and his native land, for base servitude in a strange and distant country, is daily meted out in the routine of the world to better men also, who, prevented from reaching the distant[14] homeland where dwell their unfound friends, must waste away their inner lives ineffectually in surroundings that ever remain alien and barren to them. Many a man has sufficient penetration to apprehend the inner meaning of human nature, he is prepared to discriminate its various forms and to find what is common to them,[15] but it chances that he lives in a barren wilderness or amid unfruitful luxuriance, where the everlasting monotony gives no nourishment to his spirit's needs.* Thus driven inward upon itself his imagination sickens, his spirit is forced to consume itself in dreamy fictions, for the world offers him no sustenance. It is no one's business to supply him with the sustenance he needs, or to take an interest in placing him in a more favorable atmosphere.[16] Again, many a man has a genuine impulse to create works of art, but opportunity to sift his materials, to discard carefully and successfully all that is out of keeping is denied him. Or, if his project does achieve unity and fair proportions, he may lack opportunity to give its details the last touch of perfection. Does anyone furnish what he lacks, or freely offer him counsel, or take active part in perfecting his unfinished work? On the contrary, each man must stand alone and attempt the impossible! Neither in art nor in the realization of human perfection† is there community of talent, such as was instituted long ago for the service of man's external needs! The artist becomes aware of other men's existence only when pained by criticisms irrelevant to his genius, or when their deficient understanding thwarts the effect of his own esthetic intent.[17] Thus in his highest concerns man seeks help in vain from association with his fellow-beings, and even to expect such aid is exasperating and foolish in the estimations of the elect of our age. To presage a higher, more intimate, spiritual community, to wish to promote it despite limited outlooks and petty prejudices seems to them vain romanticism.

* Cf. Schopenhauer's essay on *The Wisdom of Life*, II.

† See note on p. 19 with reference to this recurring dichotomy.

If one feels oppressed by life's limitations, they attribute it to misplaced idealism and not to life's poverty; culpable inertia, they claim, and not a lack of social encouragement is what makes a man dissatisfied with the world and disposes him to let his empty wishes roam over vast tracts of the impossible. Impossible! yes, for him whose vision is on the low plane of the present with its small horizon. What grievous doubts would assail me of man's ability to draw nearer his goal, if by weakness of imagination I were riveted to the actual and its immediate consequences.*

All who belong to a better world must for the present pine in dismal servitude! Whatever spiritual association now exists is debased in service of the earthly; aimed at some utility it confines the spirit and does violence to the inner life. When friends extend to each other the hand of fellowship, the bond should issue in something greater than each could achieve independently; each ought to grant the other full play to follow the promptings of his spirit, offering assistance only where the other feels a lack, and not insinuating his own ideas in place of his friend's. In this wise each would find life and strength in the other, and the potentialities within him would be fully realized. But what, on the other hand, comes to pass in the world? There is always some one ready to perform material service for another, even ready to sacrifice his own well-being, while to exchange knowledge,[18] to show sympathy, to mitigate sufferings, is what ranks as the

* See the development of this idea below on pp. 81-84.

highest. But there is ever an element of antipathy to the inner nature of man in ordinary friendships; people would like to have certain faults cancelled out of a friend's character, and what would be a fault in themselves they regard as such in him, too. Thus each makes sacrifice of his individuality to suit the other, until they become alike, but neither like his own true self, unless one of them has will enough to check this ruination, or unless, after long suspense between strife and concord, the friendship weakens and dissolves.[19] Woe to the man of yielding disposition, if a friend becomes attached to him! He, poor fellow, dreams of a new and stronger life, he rejoices in the happy hours which pass sweetly in this comradeship, and little does he see how his spirit becomes involved in this false felicity, and dissipates itself until at last his inner life, injured and crushed at every point, is obliterated. Many of the better sort have come to this pass, the fundamental traits of their own natures are scarcely recognizable any longer, mutilated as they are at the hand of friends and plastered all over with unnatural affectations.—Man and wife are united in tender affection, and go to build themselves a home. Even as new individuals issue from the lap of their love, so too a new and common will should develop from the harmony of their natures. Their peaceful home with its occupations, its arrangements and private joys, should reveal this will in action. Alas! that this finest of human relationships should be so universally desecrated! Its true significance remains a closed secret to those that enter into it; each keeps and cultivates his own will after marriage as before, they take turns in governing, and in silent disappointment each reckons up whether the gain really outweighs what he has sacrificed in sheer freedom. At last each becomes the other's fate, and confronting cold necessity, the ardor of their love dies out. In the last analysis, when measured by the same standard, all men's accounts come equally to nought.* Every home should be the beautiful embodiment,[20] the fine creation of a unique soul; it should have its own stamp and unique characteristics, but with a dumb monotony they are all[21] a desolate grave of freedom and true life. Does she make him happy? Does she live for him alone? Does he make her happy? Is he all complaisance? Do both count mutual sacrifice their highest joy? O torture me not, image of misery which I see deep hid behind their bliss, a sign of nearby death, the wonted deceiver who paints before them this last counterfeit of life!—What has become of the fables of ancient sages about the state?† Where is the power with which this highest level of existence should endow mankind, where the consciousness each should have of partaking in the state's reason, its imagination, and its strength? Where is devotion to this new existence[22] that man has conceived, a will to sacrifice the old individual soul rather than lose the state, a readiness to set one's life at stake rather than see the fatherland perish? Where is foresight keeping close watch lest the country be seduced and its spirit corrupted? Where find the individual character each state should have, and the

* Cf. above pp. 51-52 and note.
† The reference is probably to Plato's *Republic*.

acts that reveal it? The present generation is so far from even suspecting what this side of humanity signifies, that it dreams of reorganizing the state[23] as it does of human ideals in general; each, whether he lives in one of the old or new states, would pour all into his own mold, like some sage who lays down a model for the future in his works, and hopes that one day all mankind will venerate it as the symbol of its salvation. They all believe that the best of states is one that gives least evidence of its existence, and that permits the need for which it exists to be least in evidence also.* Whoever thus regards the greatest achievement of human art, by which man should be raised to the highest level of which he is capable, as nothing but a necessary evil, as an indispensable mechanism for covering up crime and mitigating its effects, must inevitably sense nothing but a limitation in that which is designed to enhance his life in the highest degree.

O what is the vile source of these great evils but the fact that man has no sense for anything but visible, external association, and that he wants to mold and measure everything in terms of this? In so far as association is external, it must always involve limitation. The man who would amass material possessions must grant others opportunity for doing likewise; the sphere occupied by each sets a limit to the rest, and they respect it only because they are not able to possess the world individually, but can make use of each other's persons and goods.

---

* Among other laisser-faire theorists Schleiermacher may have had Wm. von Humboldt in mind in this passage, who had stated his belief in the limitation of the state's functions in 1792. (See *Schiele,* p. 106.)

All else is concentrated upon this one end: increase in outward possessions or in knowledge, aid and protection against fate or misfortune, stronger alliances to keep rivals in check. This is all that men nowadays seek and find in friendship, marriage, and fatherland; they do not seek what they need to supplement their own efforts toward self-development, nor enrichment of the inner life. In respect to such ends every association that one enters into, from the very earliest educational ties onward, is a hindrance; at the very outset the youthful spirit, instead of enjoying free play and opportunity to see world and man as a whole, is restricted by alien ideas and early accustomed to a life of prolonged spiritual slavery.* In the midst of wealth what lamentable poverty! How unavailing is the struggle of a superior mind, seeking moral cultivation and development, with this world that recognizes only legality, that offers dead formulas in place of life, custom and routine in place of free activity, a world that boasts of great wisdom when, happily, some outworn form is discarded and gives place to something new that seems vital at the moment, but which will all too soon become a mere formula and lifeless convention in its turn. How should I find salvation in such a world were it not for you, divine

* The problem of freedom and individuality was a major consideration in Schleiermacher's educational theory. Cf. pp. 78-79, of the text, and also his lectures on pedagogy (*Werke*, III, v. 9).

His notes contain a "Catechism of reason for women of quality," the fifth commandment of which reads: "Honor the individuality and wilfullness of your children, that it may go well with them and their lives upon earth may be strong." (See *Schiele*, p. 106, and *Dilthey*, Appendix, pp. 83-84.)

imagination! Did not you give me the certain premonition of better times to come!

Yes, culture will develop out of barbarism, and life will spring even from the sleep of death! The elements of a better life are already present. Their superior potency will not remain forever in dormant hiding; sooner or later the spirit dwelling in man will arouse them into activity. As the cultivation of the earth for man's benefit is now far superior to that crude dominion over nature, wherein men fled timidly before every manifestation of her powers, so the blessed time when a true and spiritual society shall arise cannot be remote from this present childhood of humanity. The rude slave of nature would have believed nothing of a future dominion over her, nor would he have understood what had inspired the soul of one who prophesied thereof, for he lacked even the conception of this condition for which he felt no desire. Just so the man of today, if anyone holds up to him unfamiliar ideals or speaks of a different society and different relationships, cannot conceive of anything better or higher for which one could wish, nor is he at all fearful of anything ever coming to pass that would deeply put to shame his pride and indolent complacency. Yet if our present, much vaunted enlightenment developed out of a wretched barbarism, in which the germs of progress are scarcely discernible even now to a vision trained by the subsequent course of events, why should not our chaotic philistinism, amid which the eye already discerns through sinking mists the rudiments of a better world, give place at last to the sublime rule of moral and spiritual cultivation. It is coming! Why should I with faint heart count the hours which must still transpire or the generations that must pass away ere then? Why let the time of its coming trouble me, since time does not comprehend my inner life?

A man belongs to the world he helped to create; his will and his thought are all absorbed in it, and it is outside its bounds that he is a stranger. Whoever lives at peace with the present and desires nothing further is a contemporary of those semi-barbarous people who laid the foundations of our world; his life is a sequel to theirs, he is satisfied to enjoy the fulfillment of their wishes, and a better condition which they could not conceive, he does not conceive either. I, for my part, am a stranger to the life and thought of this present generation, I am a prophet-citizen of a later world, drawn thither by a vital imagination and strong faith; to it belong my every word and deed. What the present world is doing and undergoing leaves me unmoved; far below me it appears insignificant, and I can at a glance survey the confused course of its great revolutions.* Through every revolution whether in the field of science or of action it returns ever to the same point, and presenting ever the same features clearly reveals its limitations and the narrow scope of its endeavors. Its own works are impotent to advance it; they but keep it going in the same old cycle, and hence I can take no delight in them; I am not deceived into placing false

* No doubt Schleiermacher has in mind particularly the French Revolution and the Kantian revolution in philosophy. See Introduction, pp. xxi-xxxiii. Cf. also pp. 74-75, of the text.

hope in everything that appears to contain some promise. But wherever I do see a spark of the hidden fire that must sooner or later consume the outworn and recreate the world, I am drawn toward it with love and true hope as to a welcome sign of my distant home. And close at hand the sacred flame has appeared shedding its unearthly light,[24] a sign, to the knowing, that the spirit is there. All who like myself belong to the future are drawing toward each other in love and hope,[25] and each in his every word and act cements and extends a spiritual bond by which we are pledged to better times.

But this too the world makes as difficult as possible; it prevents kindred minds from recognizing each other, and contrives thus to destroy the seed of future improvement. An act, born of the most immaculate conception, is nevertheless subject to a thousand misinterpretations; it is inevitable that what has been done in the purest moral spirit should often be associated with worldly motives.[26] Too many mask themselves in false appearances to allow of confidence in everyone who shows signs of superior spirit. It is right to be sceptical of first appearances when looking for brothers in spirit; yet because the world and the times make ready confidence impossible, it often happens that two congenial spirits pass each other by unrecognized. Knowing this, take courage and have hope! You are not the only one whose roots strike into that deeper soil which at some distant time will be the surface; the seed of the future is germinating everywhere! Continue to look for it wherever possible. You will still find many a friend and will learn to recognize as such many whom you have long misjudged. And you yourself will be recognized by many; despite the world, mistrust and suspicion will at last disappear, if by the constancy of your action you give a steady token to the pure in heart. You need but impress the spirit's stamp incisively upon every action, that those who are near may discover you. Only pronounce clearly the sentiment of your heart, that those who are distant may hear!

To be sure, the world, again, has the magic of language at its command, and we have not.[27] Language has exact symbols in fine abundance for everything thought and felt in the world's sense; it is the clearest mirror of the times, a work of art revealing the current spirit. But for our purposes language is still crude and undeveloped, a poor instrument of communion.* O how long at the outset it hinders the spirit from arriving at an immediate vision of itself! Before it has yet found itself the spirit is enmeshed in the world through language, and its first difficulty is to gradually extricate itself from this entanglement. And if in spite of all the errors and corruptions introduced by words, the spirit has at last penetrated through to truth, how treacherously language then changes her tactics, now isolating and imprisoning its victim, so that he cannot communicate his discovery, nor receive further sustenance from the outside. Long must he search amid the profusion of language be-

---

* The ensuing passage on language brings out some literary conceptions of the romantic movement. Cf. especially the passage on the music of language, p. 66. See *Dilthey*, pp. 260-296; N. E. 296-331.

fore a term can be found, above all suspicion, to which his inmost thought can be entrusted; once found the unspiritual immediately catch up the phrase, give it some strange twist, so that a person hearing it thereafter must needs doubt as to its original connections. Many a word comes in answer from a distance to such an isolated soul, but he must question whether it really means what it means to him, whether it was sent by friend or foe. Is then language indeed the common possession of the children of the spirit and the children of the world! How absurd that the latter should pretend to an interest in true wisdom! No, they shall not succeed either in confusing or intimidating us! We are here waging a great battle around the sacred standard of humanity, which we, men of the future, must maintain for the coming generations. It is a decisive battle, but also a certain victory, to be won, independent of chance or fortune, by spiritual strength and genuine art.

Manners should be the outer garment worn by inner individuality,* delicately and significantly adapted to its form, revealing its fine proportions and gracefully following its movement. Always treat this consummate investiture with piety, giving it ever a lighter and finer texture, drawing it ever more closely about the self. Then must hypocrisy at length come to end, for a profane and vulgar nature appearing in the guise of nobility will soon

* The German word "Sitte," which I have here translated by "manners" has, of course, the wider meaning of one's entire "bearing," "behavior," "deportment," etc., and hence I have at times used these terms in the sequel where the same German word recurs.

be exposed. The informed observer will at every movement detect concealed defects,[28] the magic raiment will fall loosely where there is emptiness, and betray inward unshapeliness by its flutter at every rapid step. Thus the constancy and evenness of one's bearing ought to become and will become an infallible criterion of the spiritual nature within, and a token by which superior minds privately recognize each other. Language too should objectify the most interior thoughts, the highest intuitions, the most hidden observations of the spirit upon its own conduct, and the marvelous music of words should indicate the value, the degree of love, attached to each object. For though others can abuse the symbols which we consecrate to the highest, and can insinuate their petty and limited meanings where the reference is to the holy, yet is the tone of the worldling different from that of the consecrated. The same intellectual symbols dispose themselves differently and suggest a different melody to the wise than to the slaves of the age; the latter elevate something else to a first principle, and arrive at consequences that to the former are remote and strange. Each of us need only make his language thoroughly his own and artistically all of a piece, so that its derivation and modulation, its logic and its sequences, exactly represent the structure of his spirit, and the music of his speech has the accent of his heart and the keynote of his thought. If we do this, there will appear within the vulgar tongue another language, secret and holy, which the unconsecrated can neither interpret nor imitate, because the key to its characters lies in its spiritual meaning; a few phrases of his thought, a few notes of his discourse will betray the outsider.*

O if only the wise and the good might thus recognize each other by their manner and their language, if the present confusion were only dissolved and the issue clearly drawn, if the inner feud would only come to an open breach! Then victory too would draw nigh, a fairer sun would rise, for the younger generation with its open mind and unprejudiced spirit would surely incline to the better side. Significant actions can but announce the spirit's presence, and miracles must bear witness to an imprint of divine origin.† It would then be evident that the absence of beauty and unity in one's bearing, or the assuming of manners as a frigid semblance to disguise deformity, betokens deficient awareness of inner reality. It would be evident that he knows nothing about self-cultivation and has never beheld in himself the essential man, for whom the foundation-stones of language, quarried out of the inner life, have weathered and broken into small fragments; whose eloquence, designed to touch the depths, evaporates into meaningless phrases and superficial polish, while its lofty music degenerates into idle tonal artifices that are impotent to represent the real character of the spirit. No one can live simply and in the way of beauty save he who hates lifeless formulas, seeks after genuine self-cultivation, and so belongs to a world that is yet to be. No one can become a true artist in the use of language save he who sees himself with

* Cf. Introduction, pp. xvii, xxxviii, for comment on this tendency toward the esoteric in romanticism. Cf. also pp. 11-12.
† As to "miracles" cf. *On Religion,* pp. 88-89.

unclouded insight and has made the inner nature of man his own.

It is the quiet omnipotence of these sentiments, and not the criminal violence of vain experimentation, that must at last produce reverence for the highest and the dawn of a better age. May it be the aim of my life to promote such reverence, and may I thereby discharge my obligations to the world and fulfill my calling. Thus will the power I exercize combine with the efforts of all the elect, and what issues from my nature as a free activity will help mankind on the way to its true goal.

IV

PROSPECT

IS IT TRUE that we all walk the earth under the dispensation of powers not our own, and live uncertain of the future? Is it true that a heavy veil conceals every man's destiny, and that fate as a blind force, or even as the alien, arbitrary will of a higher Providence—for my purpose I see no distinction—plays with our decisions as with our desires? Certainly, if our decisions are no more than wishes, then man is the toy of chance! If he has learned to find himself nowhere but in the flux of those transient impressions and particular ideas that happen to be the realities of his life; if his whole life is preoccupied with the insecure possession of external things, and he never penetrates more deeply into his own being, because he is absorbed in dizzy contemplation of the everlasting swirl in which both he and his possessions are carried round; if under the influence of one random emotion or another his attention is always directed upon some particular external thing, which he wants to pursue or possess according to the impulse of the moment; then to be sure fate may prove hostile, robbing him of what he desires and playing with his resolutions, which deserve to be regarded as toys; then let him complain of uncertainty, since from his point of view nothing is certain; then indeed his own blindness must seem like a heavy veil, and it must surely be dark where the light of freedom does not shine; then, of course, he must want to know above all[1] whether the changes that govern him are dependent on a supreme will above all wills, or whether they are a mechanical result of the combination of many forces. For this latter possibility must terrify one who has never laid hold of his true self. If every ray of light upon the infinite chaos of things shows man more clearly that he is not a free being, but only a cog in the great wheel which moves both him and all else in its eternal revolution, then hope, renewed again and again in defiance of all experience and all knowledge, hope in a sublime mercy must be his only support.

Welcome art thou, oh cherished assurance of freedom! Every time I see the slaves of necessity trembling I welcome thee anew! Oh the beauty and peace of that clear understanding with which I confidently greet the future, knowing what it is and what it has in store; I am its master, it is not mine. It hides nothing from me; it approaches without any pretense of power over me. Only the gods,[2] who have no further scope for self-improvement, are ruled by fate, and the worst of mortals, who have no desire to perfect themselves, but not the man who is occupied, as he should be, in developing himself. Where find the limit set to my power? At what point does the dread realm of alien necessity begin? The only impossibility of which I am aware is to transcend the limits which I freely placed upon my nature from the beginning;* the only things I cannot do are those which I surrendered in deciding what I wanted to become; naught else is impossible for me save to reverse that original decision as once taken.³ Whoever regards such limitation which is the essential condition of his very existence, of his freedom, of his having a will at all, as an alien coercion seems to me strangely confused. But do I sense any further restrictions upon me within the limits of my chosen sphere? Without doubt this would be the case, if even in matters of morality and self-culture I harbored the desire for some specific result at each moment; if the performance of some particular action should at any time become in itself the object of my will, then, to be sure, this object might escape me just when I wanted it. In such a case I should indeed find myself under alien control, but were I to blame fate, I should only be mistaking the real thing at fault, namely myself. But such a fate can never befall me! For I live always in the light of my entire being. My only purpose is ever to become more fully what I am; each of my acts is but a special phase in the unfolding of this single will; and no less certain than my power to act at all is my ability to act always in this spirit; in the sequence of my actions there will be nothing unconformable to this principle. Come then what may! My will rules fate, as long as I relate everything to this compre

* Cf. pp. 28-31, for other references to this "original act of freedom." *Schiele,* pp. 106-107 has a valuable comment on the origins of this conception and of its place in the thought both of Schleiermacher and of his contemporaries, especially Fichte. The relation between individuality and limitation is also discussed on pp. xxxii, xlix, li, 127, in comparing Schleiermacher and Spinoza.

hensive purpose, and remain indifferent to external conditions and forms of life, considering them all as of equal value to me provided only that they express the nature of my being and afford new material for its inner cultivation and growth. As long as my spirit's eye keeps in view this object in its entirety,[4] seeing each particular purpose only as contained in this whole, yet truly seeing in this whole all particular aims, as long as I never drop out of mind the pursuit that I happen to interrupt, keeping my will fixed upon more than I do, relating whatever I do to all that I will, just so long does my will rule fate, and freely turn to its purposes whatever fate may bring. Such a will can never be cheated of its object, and in its very conception the idea of fate vanishes. Whence then do those changes of human fortune, which men feel to be so tyrannous, take their rise but in the fact that freedom limits freedom in a community of such wills?* Thus these changes are also an effect of freedom, and of my own freedom to boot. How could I suffer my actions to help form the vicissitudes of other men, if I did not demand that those of others should do the same for me? Yes, I do demand it most emphatically! Let time move on, and bring me what manifold materials it may for my activity, my self-development, and for the outward expression of my nature. I flinch at nothing, the order in which it comes is immaterial to me, and so are all the external conditions. Whatever the active community of mankind can produce shall pass before me, shall stir and affect me in order to be affected by me in turn,

* Cf. above pp. 17-18.

and in the manner I receive and treat it, I intend always to find my freedom and to develop my individuality through its outward expression.

Is this but a vain delusion? Does impotence hide behind this sense of freedom? Such is the interpretation which vulgar natures put upon a thing they do not understand! But this empty talk of men who debase themselves has long ago ceased to echo in my ears; between their point of view and mine the living fact renders judgment at every moment. When they see time passing, they always complain, and they tremble at an hour's approach! Through every change they pass unimproved, ever remaining the same vulgar natures that they are. But can they cite a single instance in which they might not have met the circumstances which confronted them differently? It would be easy for me to crush them still more in the midst of their troubles, forcing from them the contrite confession that the alien tyranny of which they complain is nothing but their own inertia, that they did not really want what they seemed to want, but only wished to appear desirous of it. Thus showing them the base limitations of their own consciousness and will, I might teach them to believe in a true will and true consciousness.

But whether they learn the truth or no, my own belief that I shall meet with nothing that can hinder the progress of my self-development or drive me from the goal of my endeavors, lives in me because of past acts. Ever since reason obtained the mastery of my being, and freedom and self-knowledge took up their abode in me, I have walked through diverse courses of life with this clear confidence. While enjoying the beautiful freedom of youth I succeeded in the crucial act of casting off the mummery in which long and tedious hours of educational sacrilege had clothed me;* I learned to deplore the brief independence enjoyed by the majority of men who allow themselves to be bound by new chains;† I learned to despise the contemptible efforts of the lifeless,⁵ who have forgotten even the last trace of the brief dream of freedom, who mistake what transpires in youth when freedom is just awakening and wish to keep the young faithful to old ways. In a stranger's home my sense for the beauty of human fellowship was first awakened;‡ I saw that it requires freedom to ennoble and give right expression to the delicate intimacies of human nature, which remain forever obscure to the uninitiated who respect them only as natural bans.⁶ Amid all the diversities of this world's motley spectacle I learned to discount appearances and to recognize the same reality whatever its garb, and I also learned to translate the many tongues that it acquires in various circles. Watching the great fer-

* In connection with this comment on his education in the Moravian seminary consult pp. xv-xix, and the notes on pp. 60. An interesting series of letters between Schleiermacher and his father describes the "casting off of the mummery." (*Letters*, v. 1, pp. 46-67ff.)

† Schleiermacher may be thinking in this connection of Albertini and other friends of his in the Moravian seminary, who relapsed from an abortive emancipation into permanent submission to the rule of the brotherhood. (Cf. *Schiele*, p. 107 and *Dilthey*, pp. 15-29ff.; N. E. 19-22 ff.

‡ The reference is to the home of the Dohna family in Schlobitten, where Schleiermacher was happily engaged as tutor from 1790-1793. See above pp. xxxivff. and *Dilthey*, pp. 44-61; N. E. 55-71.

ments of life, both the turbulent and the quiet ones,* I learned to understand the mentality of mankind, and how it cleaves ever to superficialities. In the quiet solitude that was my lot I looked to the inner nature of things, I took note of all purposes to which humanity is committed by its essence, and observed all dispositions of the spirit in their everlasting unity; through living contemplation I learned to assess at the right value the dead language of the schools. I have felt joy and pain, I know each sorrow and each smile, and in all that has happened to me since my real life began, is there anything from which my being did not gain strength or acquire something new, wherewith to nourish my inner life?

Let the past, therefore, be my security for the future. How can the future, being like the past, affect me differently if I remain constant to myself? I see the content of my life before me clear and fixed. I know in what respects my being has already achieved its individual form and definition, and by acting with thorough consistency on every hand, with full and undivided strength,† I shall preserve what has thus been achieved. How can I help but rejoice in novelty and in variety, which but confirms in new and ever different ways the truth

---

* I. e., the French Revolution and the intellectual changes in Germany. Cf. p. 62 and note * on the same page. See also p. xxxiii-xxxiv, with respect to Schleiermacher's "quiet solitude" during these times.

† This idea of consistent and even action occurs repeatedly (cf. pp. 42, 88) and is to be associated with the quality of equanimity that Schleiermacher says is fundamental to his character. (See p. 42) Mystics, among them Jakob Boehme, often recommend a similar even-tempered attitude toward all things.

whereof I am possessed. Am I so certain of myself that I do not require[7] such further confirmations?[8]* Am I so complete as not to welcome joy and sorrow alike, indeed whatever the world calls weal or woe, seeing that everything in its own way serves the purpose of further revealing my being's relationships? If but this be accomplished, of what importance is it that I be happy! Moreover, I also know what I have not yet made my own, I know where I am still adrift amid vague generalities and for a long time have painfully felt the lack of an individual point of view. My powers have long been busy in these directions, and some day I shall compass what is lacking, by my activity and meditations, harmonizing it inwardly with everything already mine. There are sciences which I have still to explore thoroughly, for my outlook on the world can never be complete without their knowledge. Many types of humanity are still strange to me; there are ages and peoples that I know no better than the average man does, my imagination has not in its own way entered into their thought and character, they occupy no definite place in my picture of mankind's development.† Many activities which have no place in my own being I do not understand, and I am frequently at a loss how to estimate their relation to all that is great and fine in humanity. I shall acquire all these things gradually, one with the other; the fairest prospect opens out before me.‡ What a galaxy of individuals I see

* Cf. pp. 29-34 with respect to these "confirmations."
† A very characteristic statement of the romanticist interest in history. Cf. Herder. See above pp. xxi, xxviii-xxix.
‡ "The fairest prospect": cf. title of this soliloquy.

close at hand, men so different from myself yet all of them engaged in perfecting the humanity that is in them! What an amazing number of learned men are about me, who out of pride or hospitality offer me the golden fruit of their lives in handsome jars, and the plants of distant times and places too, transplanted to the fatherland by their faithful toil!* Can fate enchain me so that I shall not be able to approach this goal of mine? Can it deny me the means of self-development, put me out of easy touch with the labors of the present generation and with the monuments of the past? Can it cast me out of this fair world in which I live into those barren wastes where contact with the rest of humanity is impossible, where vulgarity surrounds me on all sides with its everlasting monotony, and nothing lovely, nothing distinct stands out in the thick and sodden atmosphere?† To be sure, this has befallen many, yet it can not happen to me; I defy that to which thousands have succumbed. A man must sell himself in order to become a slave, and fate dares bid only for one who offers himself at a price. What is it that lures the vacillating person away from the place where his spirit prospers? What can possibly impel him to throw away the finest treasures in cowardly folly, as the fleeing warrior does his weapons?[9] It is the craving for base, ex-

* A. W. Schlegel's translations of foreign classics were cases in point.

† The leaders of the Reformed Church were anxious to get Schleiermacher away from his unchurchly companions in Berlin. In 1798 Sack had offered him a position as court-preacher in Schwedt. In 1802 events did force him to go to Stolpe. See Introduction, pp. livff. Also cf. *Letters,* v. 1, pp. 178ff. and *Schiele,* p. 108; *Dilthey,* N. E. pp. 412ff.

ternal gain,* it is the excitement of sensual desires already jaded so that the familiar draughts no longer satisfy. How could this happen to me in view of my despising such shadows! I have gained the position I occupy by industry and toil, with deliberate effort I have built a world of my own in which my spirit can flourish. How are firm connections like these to be loosened by some transient incitement whether of fear or of hope? How is some vain bagatelle to lure me from my true home and from the circle of my beloved friends?

But to continue living in this happy sphere and to become ever more closely related to it is not my only requirement; I long for another world. I still have many new ties to form; my heart must beat to the law of new loves as yet unknown to me, that the relation of these to the rest of my being may be revealed. I have experienced every kind of friendship, I have tasted the sweet joy of love with pure lips, I know what befits me in both relationships, what rule of life is appropriate to my nature. But the most sacred of all ties has yet to lift my life to a new level; some beloved soul and I must melt into one being, so that my humanity may touch other humanity in the finest of all relationships, and I may know the transfigured, higher life which will develop at this rebirth of freedom in me, the beginning of a new world for my regenerated self. I must be consecrated to paternal rights and duties, so that the maximum of power which freedom exercises over other free beings may

* A letter of Schleiermacher's to his sister (*Letters*, v. 1, p. 186) comments on the materialistic office-seeking prevalent in Berlin at the time. (See *Schiele*, p. 108.) See preceding note.

not remain dormant in me, that I may show how he who believes in freedom preserves and protects reason in the young, and how in this great problem a discerning spirit can untangle the finest maze of his and other's rights.* But will not fate overreach me just in respect to this dearest wish of my heart? Will not the world at this point take revenge upon my defiant freedom, upon my arrogant disrespect for its power? Where may she dwell with whom I might suitably link my life? Who can tell me whither I must go to seek her? For such a boon no sacrifice is too dear, no effort too great! But what if I should find her already tied, so that she hesitates to come to me?† Shall I be able to liberate her? And if I do win her, can my will decide whether as husband I shall also enjoy fatherhood?[10] Here I stand at the boundary where my will is limited by another freedom, and by the course of life, a mystery of nature. I have hope; man can do much; by strength of will and serious effort he surmounts many difficulties. But should hope and effort both prove vain, if all is denied me, am I then conquered at this point by my fate? Has it then really prevented my inner life from reaching a higher level, and succeeded by its caprice in limit-

* Cf. p. 60 and note on the same page.

† Eleonore. Schleiermacher's beloved, was married to a preacher named Grünow. This match was childless. Schleiermacher thus reflects that he is limited by "another freedom," namely the relationship between Eleonore and Grünow, and should this be surmounted, perhaps by the "mystery of nature" in respect to childbirth. These difficult circumstances, which made this love between Schleiermacher and Eleonore an unhappy one, account in some measure for the strained sentiment of the ensuing passage (pp. 78-81). See *Dilthey*, pp. 479ff.; N. E. 523ff. And *Briefe* of this period, 1800-1804.

ing my development? The impossibility of outward accomplishment does not prevent an inner process; I should pity the world more than myself and my beloved, for having lost a beautiful and rare example, a phantom that has strayed from a more perfect future into the present,[11] capable of giving warmth and life to the world's dead conceptions. As long as we belong to one another, she and I, imagination will transport us, though we have not actually met, into our lovely paradise. Not in vain have I seen the soul of woman in so many different forms, and come to know the characteristic charms of her sequestered life.* The further I still was from marriage, the greater was my care to learn the nature of its sacred domain; I know what is right there, and what is not. I have pictured to myself all its possible forms in their perfection, even as a distant, future freedom will reveal them, and I know exactly which of these forms is appropriate to me. It is thus that I also know her, the unknown love, with whom I could unite myself for life most intimately, and I am already attuned to the lovely life which we should lead together. Being obliged in my present unhappy solitude to undertake and arrange many things alone, to suppress much, and to practice much renunciation and control, in matters both great and small, there constantly hovers before me a vivid realization of how in that life all this would be different and much better. She too must surely find it so, wherever she may be, she who is so constituted that she could love me and find her satis-

* In his letters to Henriette Herz, Schleiermacher speaks of the beneficent influence of women upon his spirit. See *Letters*, v. 1, pp. 187-188ff.

faction in me. The identical longing, something far more than an indefinite desire, lifts her, as it does me, above the barren actualities for which she was not intended,* and if we should suddenly be brought together by a stroke of magic, nothing would be strange to us; we should walk easily and gracefully into our new life as if we had been engaged through fond acquaintance of long standing. And thus, even without that stroke of magic, we are not deprived inwardly of our higher life together. It is for this life and by it that we are fashioned, and only its external manifestation is lost to the world.[12]

Oh that men knew how to use this divine power of the imagination, which alone can free the spirit and place it far beyond coercion and limitation of any kind, and without which man's sphere is so narrow and precarious! How much actually touches each of us in the course of his brief life? How many sides of our nature would remain unformed and undeveloped, if man's inner life were limited to those few things with which he came into actual external contact?† Yet men are such creatures of the senses in respect to morality that they do not even trust themselves unless some overt act testifies to the truth of their feelings. He who puts such limitations on himself must live to no purpose in the great society of mankind! The opportunity to behold its life and action can be of no avail to him; helplessly he must complain of the world's dull monotony and the languor of its movements. He

* Eleonore was unhappy in her marriage to Grünow. See above p. 79 and note † on the same page.
† Cf. p. 56.

is ever wishing for new conditions, for other external provocatives to action, and looking for new friends as soon as the old have made what possible impression they could upon his soul. Life is everywhere too slow for him. But suppose it did lead him into a thousand new paths at a quicker pace, could the infinite be thus exhausted in the brief span of an individual life? What men of this type cannot even wish for, I actually achieve through the inner play of my imagination. For me imagination supplies what reality withholds; by virtue of it I can put myself in the position of any other person I notice; my spirit bestirs itself, transforms the situation to accord with its nature, and judges in imagination[13] just how it would act in such a case. To be sure, men's average judgments of other people's natures and actions are unreliable, for they reckon by some artificial rote or useless stereotype; and afterwards they act far otherwise than their previous judgments would lead them to do. But when the exercise of imagination is not merely mechanical, but accompanied by inner reflection, as it must be wherever there is true life, and when judgment is the conscious issue of such reflection, then the object contemplated,[14] though it be foreign to one's experience and only imagined, shapes the spirit, as much as if possessed by it in reality and dealt with externally. Thus in the future as in the past I shall take possession of the whole world by virtue of inner activity,* and I shall make better use of things in quiet contemplation than if I had

* See above, p. xlv for comment on this praise of the imagination.

to respond to every quickly passing impression with an overt act. Every relationship makes a deeper impression in this way, the spirit grasps it more definitely, and one's own nature is more perfectly reproduced in free, unbiased judgments. What the external life really contributes in addition is thus only a confirmation and test of an inner life which is prior and richer; the development of the spirit is not confined within the narrow limits of the external. Hence I no longer complain when my lot in the world is monotonous, nor when its course is hectic and irrational. I know that my external life will never manifest or perfect all sides of my inner nature.* It will never place me in circumstances of such magnitude that my action will decide the weal and woe of thousands, circumstances in which I could give outward proof that in comparison with one of reason's sublime and holy ideals all else is nought to me. Perhaps I shall never come into open conflict with the world and be able to show how little all that the world has power to give or to withhold can disturb my inner peace and integrity. But I myself know how I should act even in such circumstances, and I know that my spirit has long since been ready and prepared for everything of that kind. Thus, though I remain in seclusion, I nevertheless live upon the great and open stage of the world's actions. Thus, even in my solitude, I have already tied the knot with my beloved; our union is a fact, and indeed is the better part of my life. Thus, too, I shall surely keep possession of

* Schleiermacher used this idea in his Christology to criticize the view that any external revelation of Christ's nature could be complete. (See *Schiele*, p. 108.)

my only riches, the love of my friends, whatever may happen to them or to me in the future.

Men are indeed fearful that friendship will not last long, the mind seems to them fickle; a friend may change, his wonted love disappearing with his wonted disposition; loyalty is a rare treasure. And men are right. For if any of them look beyond utility in their friendships, it is the mere atmosphere surrounding a personality that they are prone to love, or perhaps some particular virtue, which they never trace to its inner root in the character, and if in the course of life's entanglements they come to miss these qualities, they are not ashamed to confess even after many years that they were mistaken in their friends.* I am not favored with a fine figure† or with anything else that is wont to catch the hearts of people at first sight, and yet everyone who has not seen into my inner nature creates for himself some superficial impression of me. Thus I come to be loved for a goodness of heart that I should not want to have, or for a modest nature which I have not got,[15] or for cleverness such as I heartily despise. This kind of love, to be sure, has often enough deserted me, and it does not belong among those riches that I prize. I consider that love alone a true possession, which my very self evokes and wins over to me anew, time and again. How could I count as my own, an affection that is called forth entirely by an impression of me due to weak discernment. I wash myself clean of any such claim, in order not to deceive these people;

* Cf. p. 45.
† On the contrary, he was small and slightly deformed. (See *Schiele*, p. 108.

but verily their false love shall not pursue me either, any longer than I can endure it. To throw them off will cost me but a single exhibition of my inner nature, one which they cannot mistake; I need but lead them straight to that which my own spirit treasures as its best, but which they cannot endure. Thus I shall rid me of this plague, that they who ought to hate me,[16] love me and consider me one of their number. I shall gladly return to them the independence which they sacrificed to a false impression. But I can always count on those who are really devoted to me, who love my inner character; my spirit holds them fast and will never forsake them. They have known me, they have looked on my soul, and if they love my spirit as it is, they must love it ever more deeply,[17] the more it develops and unfolds.

I am as certain of keeping this treasure as I am of my own being; I have never lost a friend who has been truly dear to me. You, who in the fresh bloom of youth, in the midst of a life that was strong and joyous, had to depart from our circle*— yes, I can address the dear image that dwells in my bosom, and that continues to live on in my life, in my love and in my sorrow—never has my heart forsaken you. In my thought I have imagined your development, even as it would have taken place, had you lived to see the flames that now enkindle the world;† your thinking has merged with mine, our

* The reference here is to his friend Okely, who was one of his closest companions at the Moravian seminary and who separated from the brotherhood as Schleiermacher did. Shortly after their emancipation, Okely was drowned at Northampton. See above p. xvii, also *Schiele*, p. 109, and *Dilthey*, pp. 15ff, 23, 29. † The revolutions taking place. Cf. pp. 62 and note.

love's conversation and the mutual contemplation of each other's souls never ceases, but continues to affect me as if you were living beside me as you formerly did. And you, my dear friends, who are still living in fact, though far from me, and who often send fresh impressions of your lives and thoughts, what matters distance to us?* We were together a long while and were less close to one another than we are now; for what is being together, save community of spirit? What I do not see of your lives I construct for myself; you are present to me in all things, both inward and outward, that would vitally stir your souls, and a few words between us serve to confirm my imagination or to put it on the right track where I was in chance of error. You, who are even now with me in loving comradeship, you know how little I desire to roam abroad;† I will stay in my place, and will not forego the fair opportunity of exchanging life and thought with you at every moment. Where such communion is possible, there is my paradise. If you are possessed of a different thought, well and good: distance cannot separate us.—But can death? Ah, what is death, but a greater distance?

Sombre thought, that implacably shadows all meditation upon life and the future!‡ I can assert

* This refers to Friedrich Schlegel and Dorothea Veit who had left Berlin to live together in Jena (1799). See above p. liv. and *Schiele*, p. 109, and *Dilthey*, pp. 468ff.

† The reference is particularly to his friends Henriette Herz and Eleonore Grunow. See above pp. 78-81, and *Schiele*, p. 109, and *Dilthey*, pp. 479ff.; N. E. 523ff.

‡ In a letter to his sister Schleiermacher includes a portion of this passage on death, with the following explanation: "This passage, which I have copied from a little book of mine, comes straight from my soul; it is a trifle obscure, like the whole book, but when you once understand it, it is right enough." (See *Letters*, v. 1, p. 251ff. and *Schiele*, p. 109.)

that death will never part my friends from me, for I take up their lives in mine, and their influence upon me never ceases. But it is I myself who slowly perish in their death. The life of friendship is a sequence of harmonizing chords, to a keynote which dies out when the friend passes away. Of course, within oneself reechoing tones are heard without cease for a long while and the music is carried on; but the accompanying harmony in him, of which I was the keynote, has died away, and it was this that gave me my key, just as I gave him his. What I produced in him is no more, and thereby a part of my life is lost. Every creature that loves another kills something in that other through its death, and he who loses many of his friends is finally slain himself at their hands, since cut off from influencing those who were his world, his spirit is driven inward and forced to consume itself. There are two cases in which man's end is inevitable. He must perish for whom the death of friends has irretrievably destroyed the balance between the inner and the outer life. And he too must perish for whom this balance is otherwise destroyed, he who has attained the perfection of his individuality, and in whom, therefore, no further activity is essential, even though he be surrounded by the richest of worlds. A completely perfected being is a god, it could not endure the burden of life,[18] and has no place in the world of mankind.* Death, therefore, is a necessity, and may it be the mission of my freedom to bring me nearer to this necessity. May it be my highest goal to be able to wish to die!†

* Cf. pp. 34, 48, 70.
† Cf. Novalis's *Hymnen an die Nacht,* and *Fragmentarisches.*

I wish to give myself to my friends so completely, and embrace their whole being so closely, that each may help to slay me with sweet pangs, when he leaves me, and I wish to perfect myself more and more, so that my soul may in this way also approach ever nearer the wish to die. The death of man is always the result of these two elements combined; not all my friends will leave me ere I die, nor shall I ever actually reach my goal of perfection. I shall approach my end from all sides in just proportion as befits the equipoise of my nature; of this good fortune I am assured by my perfect tranquillity[19] and my quiet contemplative life.* For a nature such as mine the highest point is reached when its inner development seeks an external embodiment, since every kind of nature in its perfection approaches its opposite.† The idea of perpetuating my inner being, and with it the whole outlook which humanity gave me, in a work of art is for me a premonition of death.[20]‡ As I first became aware of my maturity, this idea was born in me; now it waxes daily and assumes a definite form. Prematurely, I know, and yet voluntarily I shall release it from my mind, before the fire of life has died in me. For should I allow the work to ripen and grow perfect within me, my very being itself would pass away as soon as its faithful copy was ready for the world. It would have achieved its end.

* Cf. pp. 42ff. and note on p. 75.
† Cf. pp. 34, 48.
‡ Schleiermacher played with the characteristically "romantic" idea of putting his point of view into a novel, but never actually carried out the project. It would have meant "approaching his opposite," for as he says (p. 34 above), his was not the artist's imagination. Cf. pp. xxxviii-xl above, also *Schiele*, p. 109, and *Dilthey*, pp. 446ff.; N. E. 490ff.

V

YOUTH AND AGE

AS THE STROKE of the clock tolls the hours, and the sun's course measures out the years, my life, as I am well aware, draws ever nearer the hour of death. But does it also approach old age, weak and broken old age, of which everyone bitterly complains, when without warning the zest of joyous youth has slipped away, and all health of spirit, all exuberance is gone? Why do men permit life's golden years to pass, and sighing bend their necks beneath a self-imposed yoke? There was a time when I myself believed the privileges of youth did not befit manhood; I thought to conduct myself quietly and prudently, preparing for years more drab by a wise resolve of renunciation.* My spirit however, would not content itself within such narrow bounds, and I soon repented this life of bare economy. At the very first summons joyous youth returned, and ever since has held me in its protecting embrace. Were I now convinced that youth would escape me with the flight of years, I should voluntarily hasten to meet an early death, lest fear of certain misery to come embitter every good of the present, and incapacitate my life until finally I deserved an even worse end.

* Cf. *Briefe*, v. 4, pp. 16-42, for the personal experiences referred to.

But I know that this cannot be true, because it should not be. Shall the free and immeasurable life of the spirit be spent before the life of the flesh is ended, which contains the seeds of death in its very first pulsations? Shall not my imagination always contemplate beauty with its full and wonted strength? Can I not always count on buoyancy of spirit, responsiveness to good, and warmth of heart? Am I to listen with dread to the waves of time, and see them grind and channel me until I give way? Tell me, O heart, how many times the time just now spent upon this wretched thought may I still expect to live before these horrors come to pass? Could I count them, I should think a thousand times as brief as one. But be not a fool, to prophecy the spirit's strength in terms of time, for time can never be its measure! The stars in their courses do not traverse equal distances in equal times; you must seek a higher calculus to comprehend their motion. And should the spirit follow meaner laws than they? No, nor does it do so. Old age, soured, bare, and hopeless, fetches many prematurely, and some evil spirit breaks off the bud of their youth before it has scarcely blossomed; others keep their vigor long; though white, their heads are unbowed, a fire still animates their eyes, and happy laughter graces their lips. Why should I not successfully fight off the death that lurks in hiding for me, even longer than he who has maintained his prime the longest? Ignoring the toll of years and the body's decay, why should I not by sheer force of will cling to youth's dear divinity until my last breath is drawn? For what is to explain this difference in ageing, if not force of will? Is the spirit forsooth of a finite size and measure, which can be spent and exhausted? Is its strength used up by action and dissipated in every movement? Is it only misers who have been chary of their deeds that enjoy long life? If it be so, let shame and scorn smite all whose old age wears a fresh and happy look; for he deserves scorn who has been miserly with his youth.

Were time actually the measure of man's life and destiny, I should rather realize all my spiritual possibilities in a brief span; I should want to live a short life that I might keep young and vital while it lasted! What good are rays of light thinly diffused over a wide surface? There can be no revelation of power in them, no effective accomplishment. Of what avail is it to economize and conserve action, if you must weaken its inner content, and if finally you have nothing left anyway? Rather spend your life in a few years with brilliant prodigality, so that you may enjoy the sense of your strength, and be able to survey what you have amounted to. But man's measure and his destiny are not temporal; the spirit will not submit to such empirical delimitation. For what is there to break its power? What can it lose of its being by activity and by pouring itself out to others? What is there to consume it? I feel myself enriched and clarified by every action, stronger, and more sound; for in every act I receive some nourishment from humanity's common store, and in the process of growth my nature assumes a more definite character. Is this true only because I am still climbing up the hill of life? Perhaps, but when will this happy condition suddenly be reversed? When shall I begin to decline instead of growing by activity? And how will this great transformation be announced? If it comes, I can not help but recognize it, and if I recognize it, I shall rather choose to die, than to live in protracted misery, beholding in myself the impotence of human existence.*

The decline of vigor and of strength is an ill that man inflicts upon himself; old age is but an idle prejudice, an ugly fruit of the mad[1] delusion that the spirit is dependent on the body! But I know this madness, and its evil fruit shall not succeed in poisoning my healthy life. Does the spirit inhabit the fibres of my flesh, or are the two identical, that it needs must stiffen like a mummy when they are petrified? Let the body have its due. If the senses grow dull, and our impressions of reality's earthly images grow faint, then surely memory too will be dimmed, and many pleasures and delights will fade. But is this the life of the spirit? Is this the everlasting youth that I worship? If such things had power to weaken the spirit, how long had I already been old age's slave!† How long ago should I have bade my youth a last farewell! But nothing that has hitherto been unable to disturb my energetic life, shall ever succeed in doing so. Am I not surrounded by others who have sharper senses and stronger bodies? Will they not always be about me as they are now to offer the service of their love?

* Cf. *Briefe,* v. 4, p. 39 in re suicide.

† Schleiermacher in fact had to contend with certain physical handicaps, and was of the opinion he could not possibly live a long life. See *Letters,* v. 1, p. 183-184 and elsewhere. Reference is made further on to his weak eyesight.

To lament my physical decline is of all things furthest from my mind! Why should that trouble me? Would it be such a misfortune, if I did forget the events of yesterday? Are the day's minutia the world in which I live? Is the sphere of my inner life limited to the impressions I get of those particular things that happen to exist within the narrow confines of my immediate physical environment? Whoever has loved youth only because it excelled in these immediate physical advantages, and whose inferior perception cannot grasp a higher calling, may justly complain of old age and its misery. But who will dare maintain that the presence of those great and sublime thoughts which the spirit produces out of its own depths is dependent on the body, and that a sense for true reality hinges on the functioning of one's frame? In order to contemplate humanity do I need this eye, the nerve of which already begins to weaken when my life is but half over?* Or must my blood, which even now begins to flow slowly, rush more impetuously through my narrow veins, if I am to love all who deserve my love? Does the power of my will depend on the strength of my muscles, or on the marrow of my bones? Does courage depend upon my feeling in good health? Those who are thus physically favored are often enough deceived; death lurks in hidden corners, and suddenly springs upon them with sardonic laughter. What harm, then, if I already know, where my own death lies waiting? But perhaps repeated pain, or manifold sufferings, can so depress the spirit as to incapacitate it for

* See note p. 92.

its own unique and proper functions? Why! to resist such pains is also a function of the spirit; they too call forth sublime thoughts for their relief. And the spirit can find no evil in anything that merely changes its activity from one form to another.

Yes, in my advanced years I shall still have the same strength of spirit, and I shall never lose my keen zest for life. That which now rejoices me, shall ever give me joy; my will shall remain strong, and my imagination active, and nothing shall wrest from me the magic key which opens the mysterious portals of the higher world; nor shall love's ardent flame ever be quenched. I will not see the dread infirmities of old age; I vow a mighty scorn of all adversity that does not touch the aim of my existence, and I pledge myself to an eternal Youth.*

But am I not repudiating good along with evil? Is old age sheer weakness when compared with youth? Why then is it that mankind honors a grey head, even though it shows no trace of this eternal youth, freedom's finest fruit? Alas, often it is only because some people lead their lives in an atmosphere like that of a cellar, which will for a long time preserve a corpse from decay, and such men are popularly venerated as sacred bodies. People think of the soul as like a grape-vine; be it even of poor quality, it improves and is more highly prized when it grows old. Nay more! they talk much of virtues peculiar to life's riper years, of sober wisdom, cool self-possession, a rich experi-

* F. Schlegel wrote to Schleiermacher: "Youth is fleeting." (*Briefe*, v. 3, p. 84.) The latter answers, "Youth may be eternal." (Ibid., p. 89.) (Cf. *Schiele*, p. 110.)

ence, a poised and unassailable perfection in one's understanding of this variegated world. Youth's charm, they say, is only the evanescent blossom of human nature, but the mature fruit is old age and what it brings the soul. Then only are the innermost depths of human nature ripe for enjoyment when they have been completely purified by air and sun, and brought to some significant and beautiful perfection. O ye northern barbarians, who do not know the happier clime, where fruit and blossom burst forth together, and race side by side in all their glory to a joint fulfillment!* Is the world so cold and unfriendly that the human spirit may not emulate this higher beauty and perfection? Of course, everyone cannot have all that is good and beautiful, but diverse gifts are given to diverse persons and not apportioned to the different seasons of life. Each man is a plant of unique growth, but he can continually bear fruit and flower at the same time according to his kind. Whatever can be harmoniously realized in a single individual, he can cultivate simultaneously and possess permanently; he not only can but should.

How does man acquire discreet wisdom and ripe experience? Are they granted him from on high, and is it foreordained that he shall not receive them until he can prove that youth is passed? I am conscious of acquiring them at this very moment; it is precisely the urge of youth and the quickened life of the spirit that brings them forth. To inspect all

* The appeal of Italy! Cf. Goethe's Mignon, and Faust; also Nietzsche's treatment of the antithesis between northern and Mediterranean culture that runs through German history and thought.

things, to absorb them in the innermost sense, to master the force of random emotions lest tears either of joy or grief dim the spirit's vision or cloud its impressions, to proceed readily from one thing to another, and being of insatiable energy to assimilate even the experience of others by rehearsing their deeds in imagination, such is the active life of youth, and such too is the process by which wisdom and experience come into being. The livelier the imagination, the more active the spirit, the more is their growth hastened and prospered. And when they have been acquired, is the vigorous life that produced them no longer appropriate? Are then these supreme virtues ever perfected? If they were born in youth and by reason of youth, will they not always require the same energy to maintain and further their growth? Mankind, however, is deceived by a hypocritical vanity in respect to this its greatest blessing, and its hypocrisy is rooted in depths of narrowest ignorance. Youth's restlessness is supposed to imply the urge of a seeker, and seeking is not thought becoming to one who has reached the end of life; such a one should clothe himself in the repose of idleness,[2] that respected symbol of life's fulfillment, and in emptiness of desire,[3] the sign of complete understanding. Such should be the deportment of old age, they say, lest seeming still to be a seeker, man descend into the grave amid laughter mocking his vain efforts.[4] But only those who have sought what is cheap and vulgar may pride themselves on having found all they desire! What I aspire to know and make my own is infinite, and only in an infinite series of attempts can I completely fashion my own being. The spirit that drives man forward, and the constant appeal of new goals, that can never be satisfied by past achievements, shall never depart from me. It is man's[5] peculiar pride, to know that his goal is infinite, and yet never to halt on his way, to know that at some point on his journey he will be engulfed, and yet when he sees that point, to make no change either in himself or in his circumstances, nor in any wise to slacken his pace. Hence it is fitting that he should ever pursue his way in the carefree buoyancy of youth. I shall never consider myself old until I am perfect, and I shall never be perfect, because I know and desire what I should. Furthermore, the excellences of old age cannot conflict with those of youth, for not only do the qualities esteemed in old age develop in youth, but old age in its turn nourishes the young and tender life. It is generally conceded that youth fares better when ripe old age takes an interest in it, and in the same way a man's own inner youth is enhanced, if he acquires in early life the spiritual qualities of maturity. A practiced eye surveys its field more quickly, and a person of experience grasps a situation[6] more readily, and that love which springs from a higher level of self-development must needs be more intense. Wherefore I shall preserve my youthful vigor and I shall enjoy its zest unto the last. Unto the last I shall gain in strength and in vitality with every act, and with each step in my self-development I shall become more capable of love. I shall marry my youth to my old age, that the latter too may enjoy exuberance and be permeated with vivifying warmth. For what is it, after all, of which men complain in old age? not of consequences that necessarily follow from experience, wisdom, and self-development. Does a treasury of accumulated ideas make a man less sensitive, so that nothing either old or new interests him? Do established words of wisdom at last give way to disquieting doubts that vitiate all action? Is self-development a consuming fire that leaves the soul an inert mass? The general complaint is only that youth has fled. And why does youth fail man? Because in his youth he has lacked maturity. Let there be a double marriage. Let the strength of years enter into your robust spirit at once to preserve its youth, that in later years youth may protect you against the weakness of old age. The usual division of life into youth and age ought never to be made. He debases himself who wishes first to be young, and then old, who allows himself to be controlled first by what is called the spirit of youth, and only afterwards wishes to follow what is considered the counsel of maturity. Life cannot bear this separation of its elements. There is a two-fold activity of the spirit that should exist in its entirety at every time of life, and it is the perfection of human development ever to become more intimately and more clearly conscious of both its aspects, assigning to each its own peculiar and proper function.

The individual existence of a plant is perfected in its blossom, but the world attaches supreme value to its fruit, which serves as protection to the seed of future generations, and is a gift which every

creature must offer in order that the rest of nature may receive his life. So too, the supreme thing for a human being is the spirited life of youth, and woe to him whom it forsakes, but the world desires him to grow old, that his life may bear fruit, the sooner the better. Wherefore set your life in accord with this fact once and for all. It is a lesson which old age teaches men all too late, when time has dragged them thither in its chains, but by a firm resolution of your free will you may at once make it your rule in all matters upon which the world has a claim. Wherever fruit appears as the spontaneous result of your life's free flowering, let it develop to the world's advantage, and may there be hidden in it a fertile seed destined to unfold one day into a new life of its own. But let whatever you offer to the world be fruit.[7] Do not sacrifice the least part of your being itself in mistaken generosity! Let no bud be broken off, nor the smallest leaf plucked, through which you receive nourishment from the surrounding world! On the other hand, do not put forth mere foliage,[8] unpruned and unpleasing, in which some poisonous insect may hide and sting you. If it is not part of your own proper development, or the growth of new members, let it be genuine fruit, engendered within the heart of the spirit, a free act testifying to its youthful creative energy.*
But when it is once conceived, such fruit should emerge from the province of the inner life; then let

---

* Adopting Schleiermacher's distinction between fruit and blossom, one may say that his *Speeches on Religion* were fruit of his life, the *Soliloquies* blossom. And they appeared almost simultaneously, as in that "happy clime" (see p. 95 above)! See also Introduction, p. xlvi.

its further development conform to the laws of outward behavior. Then let shrewdness and sober wisdom and cool discretion take it in charge, that what your love generously intended for the world may actually prove to its benefit. Then weigh means and end with care, take heed and be circumspect with cautious misgiving, seek counsel of work and power, despise no pains, and wait for propitious moments with untiring patience.

Woe unto me, if my youth, with its vitality that brooks no restraint and its restless imagination, should ever meddle with the affairs of old age, and failing to succeed in the realm of action, which is not its proper province, should thereby waste the strength of its inner life! Only such as are ignorant of inner energies[9] may perish thus, those who, misunderstanding the spiritual urge, wish to be young in their outward behavior. They expect fruit to ripen in a moment even as a blossom opens in a night; each of their projects crowds upon the heels of another, and none matures. Every enterprise, which they commence, is destroyed in the rapid alternation of their conflicting plans. And when they have thus wasted the loveliest half of life in vain attempts, doing and achieving nought, because to do and to accomplish was their only aim, then they condemn the free imagination and the youthful life. Nought but old age is left them, weak and miserable as it must be, wherever youth has been used up and driven out. Lest it flee from me also, I shall not abuse it; I shall not expect its service in matters that are not its proper sphere; I shall keep it within the limits of its own domain, that it may meet with no injury. But there in truth it shall have full sway, now and forever in unmolested freedom, nor shall any law, the proper sphere of which is to govern external actions, cramp my inner life.

May my inner activity and all that affects it, in so far as the world has no claim upon it and it concerns only my own growth, bear youth's colors everlastingly, and may it proceed wholly from an inner impulse with a gracious and perfect joy. O my soul, let no rule be imposed on your coming in and going out, your hours of meditation and reflection! Heartily despise such alien legislation and banish the thought which would put the free movement of your life under the sign of a dead letter. Let no one persuade you that one thing must wait upon the completion of another! Proceed, if you like, with buoyant step; what you have done lives on in you, and you will find it again when you return. Do not anxiously ponder what to begin and what will come of it! You alone are in the making, and whatever you can will, is also part of you.[10] Shun frugal behavior! Let life be unconfined: no power is ever lost, unless you repress it within yourself, and leave it unused. Let not your will for today be determined by your wish for tomorrow! Take shame, free spirit that you are, if ought within you should become subservient to the rest; no part of your being may be mere means to an end, for one is as precious as another. Wherefore whatever you become, let it be for its own sake. A stupid self-deception to think that you ought to want what you do not want! Let not the world tell you how you should serve it and when! Laugh to scorn its silly pretensions, spirited youth, and do not brook restraint. Whatever you give is a gift of your freedom, for the resolve to benefit the world must issue from within you. Attempt nothing unless it proceeds freely from a love and desire within your soul. And let no limit be set upon your love, no measure whether of kind or of duration! If it is your own, who can demand it of you? Is not its law entirely within you? Then who may command it in any respect? Be ashamed to depend on other's opinions in such matters of holiest import. Blush for that false shame which fears lest people may not understand you when you reply to the questioner: "Such is the reason of my love." Let not yourself be troubled in the fullness and joy of your inner life by anything external whatsoever! Who would choose to combine within himself elements that are incompatible, and thus be soured in his soul? Grieve not for what you cannot be or do! Who would be ever gazing toward the impossible in empty aspiration and turning covetous eyes upon goods that are not his?

Thus is my inner life joyous and untrammelled! And how should time and destiny ever teach me another philosophy? I give the world its due; in my outward behavior I strive for order and wisdom, discretion and proportion. Indeed, what reason have I to disdain anything that proceeds so readily and freely and happily from my inner being and its activity? By observing the world one will gain all this in rich measure without effort. But in beholding himself, man triumphs over discouragement and weakness, for from the consciousness of inner freedom there blossoms eternal youth and joy. On these have I laid hold, nor shall I ever give them up, and so I can see with a smile my eyes growing dim, and my blond locks turning white. Nought can happen to affright my heart, and the pulse of my inner life will beat with vigor until **death.**

SCHLEIERMACHER'S REVISIONS OF THE SOLILOQUIES

In the second and third editions of the *Soliloquies,* 1810 and 1822, Schleiermacher made significant changes in the text. Passages so changed are indicated by numerals in my translation, which follows the first edition, and the corresponding changes are now given here. pp. 104-112.

As explained in the Preface (pp. v-vi) I have included only such revisions of the text as involve material changes in the meaning, omitting all changes which Schleiermacher seems to have made for purely stylistic reasons, since the literary significance of these would tend to be modified, if not lost, in translation.

I am entirely indebted to F. M. Schiele's critical edition of the *Monologen* (referred to as *Schiele*) for the detailed comparison of Schleiermacher's three versions involved in these notes, and with slight modifications the following system of signs, used in citing the changes, has also been borrowed from him.

A Original text of 1800.
B Text of 1810.
C Text of 1822.

The portion of A modified in B and C is printed in italics. If the change is a substitution made in both B and C, the substituted passage follows immediately upon the italicized passage without intervening signs. If the substitution occurs only in B, then the sign B intervenes, if only in C, then C. Additions are indicated by italicizing the word which immediately precedes them, and then printing: B, or C, or BC (when both) adds. Deletions are indicated by italicizing the deleted passage and following it with the words: Omit from B, or C, or BC.

OFFERING

[1] *No choicer*—No more confidential.

[2] *The highest*—The most intimate.

[3] *Enduring . . . granted you*—Dependable, for throughout life you will know the joy, which this pure insight into a fellow-being has aroused.

[4] *Thought*—Murmuring.

REFLECTION

[5] *Very natural*—Oft recurring.
[6] *Life*—C adds: revealing all the hidden springs of action.
[7] *Whole*—Essential.
[8] *Become . . . Eternal*—C: attain an immediate awareness of your relations to the Infinite and Eternal.
[9] *Like . . . grave*—With gloomy fanaticism, like unto that which kills wives or slaves beside a husband's grave.
[10] *Know*—C: find therein.
[11] *Greatest pleasures*—(I have here followed C in the text above as giving the most consistent sense). A and B read: "good therein."
[12] *To create . . . beauty*—To make of his life something charming and admirable.
[13] *Their . . . ear*—C: I am given to understand their sense of life as like the mood of an untrained listener . . . his ear . . .
[14] *A permanent creation*—Like the artist's instrument (C: voice) whence that harmony proceeds.
[15] *Only*—I have a clear vision of.
[16] *Is free* (omit).
[17] *Transmuted . . . life*—Viewed as part of a free, inner life.
[18] *Knows*—C adds: well how to distinguish.
[19] *What man . . . world*—Self and not-self, alike in his life and in the world.
[20] *What the . . . primary*—To the multitude the external world, the world emptied of spirit, is the primary and greatest reality.
[21] *To me . . . reflected*—For me the spirit, the inner world, opposes itself boldly to the outer world, the realm of matter, of things. Does not the spirit's union with a body point to its greater union with everything corporeal? Do I not grasp the outer world by force of my senses? Do I not carry the eternal forms of things forever within me? And hence, do I not recognize these things only by the reflected light of my inner being?
[22] *Is there . . . conscious thereof?* (omit from BC).
[23] *All those . . . free doing*—Thus for me the earth is the stage of my own free activity, and in every feeling, however much the outer world may seem to force it on me, in those feelings too wherein I sense the kinship of material existence with Universal Being, there is free, inner action on my part. [The point here is that even in the religious feelings of absolute dependence man's soul is active and not entirely passive. See pp. 141-142, 154. (Slight differences exist between B and C here.)]

24 *Every real . . . knead me*—There is always some influence passing from me to it also, and I do not feel myself limited by it in any different sense than by my own body. But what I truly regard as existing independently of me and limiting me as a finite and particular being, what I consider to be the real world endowed with omnipresence and omnipotence, is the eternal community of spiritual beings, their influence upon each other, their mutual development, the sublime harmony of freedom. And it is fitting that this reality should fashion and transform the surface of my being. This heavenly world alone shall mold me.

25 *World*—C adds: of spiritual beings.
26 *Perceptions I have*—Elements.
27 *Holy*—C: happy.
28 *Plays the melody*—Sets the harmony.
29 *But*—To be sure.
30 *It indicates . . . I do.*—It determines what results are still possible and what not, but it does not determine the intrinsic strength of my effort to secure them.

31 *Whether external . . . activity*—(I have inserted this clause from B and C in order to bring out the meaning of A better.)
32 *Objective result*—Valid for others, too.
33 *An illusion . . . necessity*—A mask behind which there hides sometimes a comic and then again a tragic, deceptive necessity.

34 *Reveals . . . being*—Refers me to my being in its entirety.
35 *Without being . . . nature*—C: without longing to lose himself in thinking of the infinite realm of being in all its forms and gradations?

36 *Spirit's action*—C: life of the spirit.
37 *Perhaps*—For many.
38 *Ultimate . . . thought*—C: depths of meditation.
39 *Intimate* (this from B and C). A: sacred.
40 *Consideration*—C: contemplation.
41 *In what . . . acting*—Observe the form and limit appropriate to your action.

42 *The spirit . . . but itself*—The spirit creates its world by the force of its will, and the activity, which manifests itself in the variety of its creation, is one of purest freedom; at rest in action, ever conscious of its immutable identity, it leads a blessed life. For therein it requires nothing but itself, and its . . ..

43 *Lamenting*—Believing.

SOUNDINGS

[1] *Certain*—C adds: but tries to reckon entirely with unknown quantities.

[2] *The inevitable*—C: A constant.

[3] *What is truly human*—C: reason.

[4] *Those feelings . . . brutes*—The lower feelings and impressions, renouncing those that are most distinctive of humanity.

[5] *Precincts*—B and C add: and losing true self-respect.

[6] *Circle of humanity*—C: community he deserted.

[7] *Discovered humanity*—C: received the vision of humanity.

[8] *Humanity*—C: reason.

[9] *Into . . . brutishness*—C: to the unconnected and confused impressions of animal sense.

[10] *Humanity*—C: life.

[11] *By reason of his*—In so far as each has his own.

[12] *That man*—C: that the inner man.

[13] *Of one . . . same*—In each case like unto all other individuals.

[14] *Thus . . . mankind*—Thus man's awakening is ever gradual and not always complete.

[15] *Rising to*—C: looking up to.

[16] *Which . . . herself*—With the development of which freedom has identified herself.

[17] *Expressing . . . higher being*—C: revealing to be sure all the elements of humanity, but only in a crude mass, like a mineral which has lacked the conditions for its characteristic crystallization, if they have not grasped the idea of individual uniqueness.

[18] *To view . . . friction*—That humanity should exist merely as a homogeneous mass, split up externally to be sure into units, but these all inwardly alike. I was incredulous that the spiritual uniqueness of individuals should be a merely transient phenomenon produced by external contacts and frictions, but without any inner foundation. (There are minor variations in B and C. See pp. 123, 126ff., 138ff. for the development of this theme: the basis of individuality in Schleiermacher's thought.)

[19] *All*—C: all variations.

[20] *Alone*—C: in particular.

[21] *Whether . . . from it*—Whether he may to a certain extent separate his individual being again from universal humanity. (There are minor differences between B and C.)

[22] *Knowing it?*—B and C add: What often appears to be such an inner change is certainly either mere appearance,

caused by a change in outward circumstances, or else it is a correction of our first impressions, revealing more deeply the inner nature of someone whom we had at first misjudged through haste. (C adds further) But as for my own self-knowledge, above all.

[23] *Are concealed*—C: are harmoniously concealed.

[24] *I am convinced . . . seldom reaches*—Of all differences in human behavior and vocation, which reveal differences in men's natures too, the one that strikes me most, as being pertinent to my own case, is the following. There is too great a contrast between developing one's inner humanity into distinctness by manifold activity, on the one hand, and on the other, projecting it into works of art which clearly convey to everyone what one is trying to express, for both of these gifts to be granted to the same individual in an equal measure. (Cf. pp. 87-88.) Of course, he who is still in the outer court of moral development, who fears as an initiate to limit himself by firm decision, will like to combine something of both in his crude essays at life with the result that he will not go far in either direction. Most lives are in this state of indetermination. But whoever has entered a little further into the sanctuary of morality will soon attach a preference to one of these two courses, and will preserve but few connections with the other. Not till the very end of life's development do the two again seem to approach each other, and to combine them is the privilege of a perfection that man seldom reaches.

[25] *Observation*—C adds: of others.

[26] *To my thought*—To my own impulses. (Then C adds): I behold what the artist does with reverence, but . . ..

[27] *I like*—C: I abandon myself to.

[28] *I do . . . expressed*—C: And if I must of necessity express my thoughts, I am never concerned to eliminate every trace of a refractory element in my materials and to produce something perfect, as the artist is.

[29] *Learns*—B adds: in quiet meditation.

[30] *In order*—Not only.

[31] *Ever determining*—But also to determine.

[32] *If*—C: as far as.

[33] *I . . . otherwise*—C: I no longer expect to ever get beyond it.

[34] *Realize themselves*—C adds: to absorb spiritually all that surrounds them.

[35] *Next act*—C: future acts.

[36] *Highest*—First. (C begins a new paragraph with this sentence.)

[37] *Those*—C: Those of my friends.

[38] *Science*—B and C add: except incidentally.

[39] *The slavery . . . began*—slavery to alien influences.

⁴⁰ *But whatever . . . being*—C: but less than other men will I have to retrace my steps, for whatever I do embrace will have become my own and will bear my impress. Whatever part of the world I am permitted to understand will by this course be reconstructed within me and taken up into my being.

⁴¹ *Inner*—C: acquired.

⁴² *This outward . . . belongs*—This outward side of him has little to do with my love for him, which does not feed upon this, nor is as much excited and rejoiced thereat as in the case of those who do not previously know the inner man. My expectancy is not so tense in regard to his acts as is theirs for whom everything depends upon successful results. All this . . ..

⁴³ *Source*—C adds: that they have never been aimed at merely pleasing, and still less motivated by stubborn partisanship.

⁴⁴ *They are*—C adds: never have I been so overwhelmed by congeniality in particular respects as to deceive myself about deeper inner differences.

⁴⁵ *Opposites . . . each other*—Those whose paths are far apart approach one another.

⁴⁶ *A person . . . neighborhood.*—The more his mind aspires to universality, the more a man engaged in self-culture feels attracted by various spheres, and people who are rooted in one or another of them are thus led to think he belongs with them. The more individualized I become, the more need a person will have for comprehensive appreciation and for an outgoing love toward character that is different from his own, if his understanding of me and his attachment is to be permanent.

THE WORLD

¹ *Reason*—C: understanding.

² *From above*—C: is it, one wonders, from above or from below?

³ *His own service*—For the service of his outward existence.

⁴ *The strength of his spirit*—The power of his mind over matter.

⁵ *The consciousness . . . body*—An unwonted sense of physical power.

⁶ *The concept*—C: the realm.

⁷ *The work*—C: the common work.

⁸ *Perfection!*—B and C add: To what purpose is an increased power over physical nature if it does not promote the life of one's spirit? Why boast of your outward co-operation if it does not promote spiritual community? Health and strength are, to be sure, great goods, but do you not despise him who only wants to make an exhibition of them?

110   SCHLEIERMACHER'S SOLILOQUIES

⁹ *Companion*—C: friend.
¹⁰ *Elevating*—B and C add: by the image of a love, to whom he could devote himself and in whom he could find full life.
¹¹ The order of sentences from here on through line .... on page ... is radically altered in B and C, and there are considerable additions. The sequence is as follows: after *mutual longing*. B and C add: For man is still bound by his outward station, by the place which, in the meagre thing we call society, is assigned to him, but which he can not win for himself, and men cling to these restricting ties more tenaciously than a plant to mother earth. (Cf. p. 32.) Why so? Because it costs them little, they think, to cramp the higher spiritual life in order to be more certain of enjoying the lower. This is why they allow no free association to prosper, no open, spontaneous life; this is why they live so strangely, almost hermit-like, in close little cells, next to each other but not with each other; this is why they avoid union on a great scale, making but a miserable counterfeit of it in a federation of small states, and just as the fatherland is ridiculously divided, so is each of their little communities. [Cf. pp. 58-59, a propos the ideal of German unity.]

After this in B and C there follows the passage on page 54-55. *Many a man has sufficient penetration . . . favorable atmosphere*. But the last part of this passage is changed as shown in the notes on page 110 below.

After this there follows (p. 54): *The piteous fate of the negro . . . barren to them* (p. 54).

Then (p. 55): *Again, many a man has a genuine . . . association with his fellow-beings;* (p. 55). With changes as given in the notes on p. 110

Then (p. 54): *The earth's resources . . . is no one's business* (p. 54).

Finally (p. 55): *And even to expect such aid . . . its immediate consequences* (p. 56). Cf. *Schiele*, pp. 53-54.

¹² *I*—A fortunate man.
¹³ *But no means . . . inner life*. But few are able to find the spiritual companions who can cause their inner lives to prosper.
¹⁴ *The distant*—Their true.
¹⁵ *And to find . . . them*—Or to absorb the very nature of it and enter into its secrets with loving adaptation.
¹⁶ *For the world . . . favorable atmosphere*—His creative powers are spent in unhappy experiments; for no propitious winds waft him into a more favorable clime, he can reach no helpful friend, whose business it would be to supply him with the sustenance he needs, and to lead him to fruitful sources of knowledge.
¹⁷ *In the pain . . . esthetic intent.*—C: when they criticize what is alien to their spirits in his work, and he is obliged to experience that his own esthetic purposes are obstructed, be-

cause they demand something foreign to his genius.
[18] *Knowledge*—experiences and insights.
[19] *The friendship*—C: the false friendship.
[20] *The beautiful*—C: the most beautiful.
[21] *Are all*—C: almost all become.
[22] *New existence*—Higher existence. [The terms "new" and "old" were appropriate here in view of the rising national sentiment in Germany. Schleiermacher's strong participation in this sentiment is evidenced not only by ensuing passages in the text, but also in his letters (see *Letters*, v. 2, pp. 57-58ff.) and by his public career. See Introduction, pp. lviff.
[23] *The state*—C: society. [The change in wording here is indicative of Schleiermacher's increasing political liberalism in face of the Metternich reaction. See Introduction, pp. lviff.
[24] *Light*—C adds: an awful warning to the superstitious slaves of the present.
[25] *All . . . are drawing, etc.*—C: May all . . . draw, etc.
[26] *Worldly motives*—C: impure worldly motives.
[27] *At its command . . . not*—C: more at its command than we have.
[28] *Concealed defects*—C: the true shape and strength of limbs though concealed.

PROSPECT

[1] *He must want . . . above all*—He must strive to know, albeit in vain since the alternatives as he imagines them are inconceivable.
[2] *The gods*—B and C add: of mythology.
[3] *I surrendered . . . once taken*—Contradict what I then did; but how could I wish to reverse that original decision by virtue of which I am what I am.
[4] *Its entirety*—C adds: to the exclusion of all else.
[5] *The lifeless*—C: those who even in their prime are lifeless.
[6] *Respect . . . bans*—C: who often endure them as natural restrictions more than they respect them.
[7] *Do not*—No longer.
[8] *Confirmations . . . to welcome*—C adds: but am entitled to enjoy changeless peace. No I shall ever welcome.
[9] *As the fleeing . . . weapons*—As the seaman in a raging storm casts overboard the cargo.
[10] *Can my will . . . fatherhood*—Does not the incomprehensible often make sport of the dearest and truest love, and prevent a husband from also enjoying fatherhood?
[11] *Has strayed*—B and C add: from days of pristine virtue or.
[12] *To*—C adds: us and to.

[13] *Judges*—C adds: confidently.
[14] *When judgment . . . contemplated*—C: when the act imagined is a conscious outcome of such habitual reflection, then this act, . . .
[15] *I have not got*—C: is not at all as they imagine it.
[16] *To hate me*—C: to turn from me.
[17] *More deeply*—B and C add: and genuinely.
[18] *Could*—Can.
[19] *Perfect*—Inward.
[20] *A premonition*—Like a premonition.

YOUTH AND AGE

[1] *Mad*—C: Sad.
[2] *Idleness*—C: wisdom.
[3] *Emptiness of desire*—C: peace of heart.
[4] *Efforts*, C adds: But what they call the repose of wisdom is only idleness, and their peace of heart is an empty peace.
[5] *It is man's*—C: Let it be my . . . my goal . . . etc.
[6] *A situation*—C: everything.
[7] *Fruit*—C adds: that is ready to fall.
[8] *Mere foliage*—C: the unsatisfying outgrowth of a turbulent disposition.
[9] *Inner energies*—C: life's richer possibilities.
[10] *Part of you*—C: part of your life.

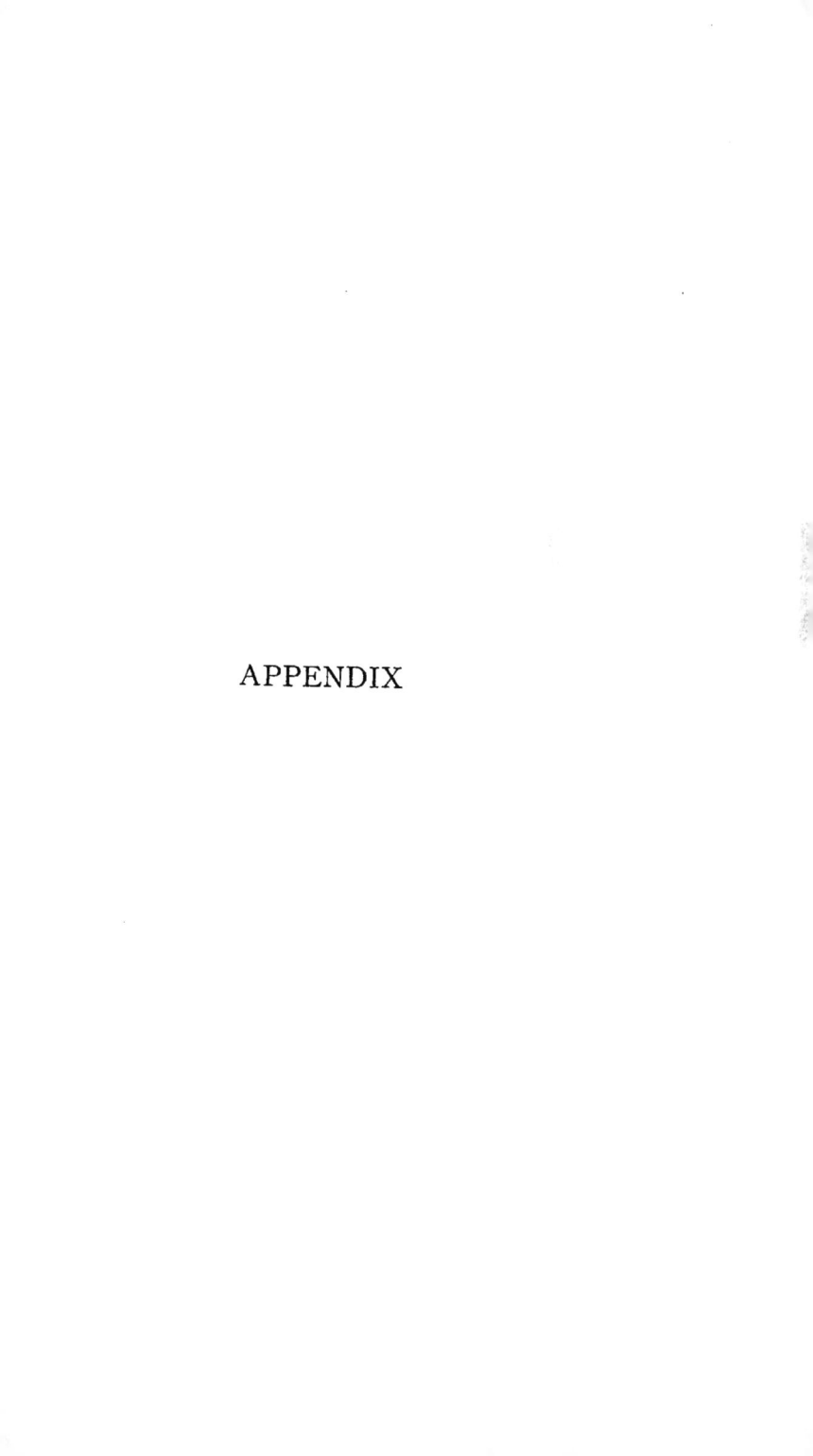

APPENDIX

APPENDIX
I

THE DEVELOPMENT OF SCHLEIERMACHER'S PHILOSOPHICAL SYSTEM

Schleiermacher's intellectual life until about 1792 was that of the youthful philosopher, whose immature intelligence moves amid generalities with significant instinct and logical acumen, but without critical self-possession. The years that immediately followed from 1792 to 1802, were the years that brought him his fundamental insights, and that also saw the first expression of these in the *Speeches on Religion* (1799) and the *Soliloquies* (1800). The further development, the manifold application, and the systematic formulation of what he took these insights to mean occupied him throughout the remainder of his life. This appendix will trace the development of his ideas in the first and third of these periods in some detail, but will pass more briefly over the second, despite its greater importance, because Schleiermacher's own interpretation of this second period is given in the text of the *Soliloquies*, and I have already given mine in the Introduction (pp. xi-lx above).

Sec. 1. *Earliest Manuscripts* (1789-1793).

Before he commenced to write at all, Schleiermacher had been "nursed in the womb of piety" at home and in Moravian schools.[1] He had also separated from the Moravian Botherhood when he felt that to continue in its limited ways of life and thought would be to wear a "false mask."[2] He had become devoted to classical studies. Finally, he had begun to study the philosophers, principally Aristotle, Kant, Leibniz and Spinoza at first. The trend of these first philosophic studies can be inferred in the main from certain extant manuscripts which Wilhelm Dilthey examined, and in part published in an appendix to his *Life of Schleiermacher*. The manuscripts date, he believes, from the time of Schleiermacher's initial philosophic studies at Halle and shortly thereafter.[3]

In these papers Schleiermacher appears to be wrestling, chiefly with Kantian philosophy, as with a veiled destiny, to win his own spiritual integrity. In what is presumably the earliest of them all. *Über das höchste Gut*, he accepts the Kantian definition of the *summum bonum* as morality plus happiness, together with Kant's criticism of hedonistic ethics and conception of the moral law as a categorical principle of pure practical reason.[4] Yet these formulations disturb him. He thinks the moral law should be related to the *summum bonum* as an algebraic equation is related to the geometrical curve described in accord-

[1] *On Religion*, p. 9.
[2] See pp. 73-74.
[3] *Dilthey*, Appendix, pp. 1-145. These pages are the primary source, in print, of our knowledge of Schleiermacher's philosophy in its beginnings. For some of the early manuscripts, however, a fuller text is to be found published elsewhere. (See notes 8-11 on p. 118.)
[4] See *Dilthey*, Appendix, pp. 6-19. Dilthey dates this paper 1789 Schleiermacher's last year as a student at Halle.

ance with it.[5] It seems to him unreasonable for a moral law to enjoin conduct that surrenders a real part of the highest good. Being unable, however, at this time to formulate a more satisfying moral principle than Kant's, Schleiermacher contents himself in this initial essay with a criticism of the theological postulates which Kant attaches to his ethics. He objects to the idea that morality requires belief in a God able to provide the perfect union of morality and happiness. A "good will," the only essential requirement of morality, is not only possible, but all the purer if independent of such belief. Moreover, it is questionable whether even a God could unite what Kant has put asunder! If man remains a creature of the senses, will not deviations from the Kantian law of reason be inevitable even in paradise? On the other hand, if he be divested of his sensibility in the world beyond, will he then be capable of what Kant calls happiness?

Thus, at the very beginning of his philosophical career Schleiermacher rejected the attempt to found theism on moral considerations. An entry in his diary some years later reads: "Religion must be justified on its own account."[6] In a letter to his friend Brinkmann (1789) he speaks of forwarding a manuscript of one hundred pages *On Religion*.[7] Unfortunately, this manuscript has been lost, so that we do not know how far Schleiermacher's thought on religion had ad-

[5] *Dilthey*, Appendix, p. 9. Schleiermacher repeats this idea in later writings (see *Werke*, III, v. 2, pp. 357ff., 446ff.) and it became a cardinal tenet of his, in contrast to Kant, that the good and not the moral law is the controlling concept in moral philosophy. The idea may originally have been suggested to him by the work he did as a pupil of Eberhard's, translating portions of Aristotle *Ethics* (see p. xix above).

[6] *Dilthey*, Appendix, p. 101.

[7] *Briefe*, v. 4, p. 3, and also *Dilthey*, Appendix, p. 4.

vanced, before he joined the Berlin romanticists in 1796, toward the ideas expressed in his *Speeches on Religion* in 1799. The steps leading up to the *Soliloquies* of 1800 are easier to trace.

There is a New Year's sermon of 1792 and also an essay in manuscript called *Über den Wert des Lebens,* which Dilthey dates 1793, both of which anticipate many parts of the *Soliloquies* in idea and in language.[8] In the essay Schleiermacher continues his search for a more satisfactory ideal of life than that furnished in Kant's philosophy. The dualism between pure practical reason and happiness is still troubling him, and while he is as yet unable to resolve it, he is more than ever convinced that some ideal sense of life (*eine gewisse Idealempfindung des Lebens*) can be found which will do justice to both aspects of human desire.[9] "I must seek to know the truth about my life," he says . . . "For I have long been comforted by the firm belief that Truth and Happiness are one." . . . "There shall be no cleft in me between appetite and understanding; they shall be one."[10] What the ideal sense of life is, in which these oppositions are overcome, Schleiermacher cannot say, but he suggests that a consideration of man's distinctive powers of thinking, feeling, and willing and of their harmonious development may be the path of moral discovery.[11] In any case, the human ideal is to be found in man

[8] See pp. xxxix-xli above for further comment on this fact. Comparison of the three is facilitated by using Schiele's edition of the *Monologen*, which contains both the sermon and the earlier essay in an Appendix, pp. 147-198.

[9] *Dilthey,* Appendix, p. 50, or *Schiele,* p. 175.

[10] *Dilthey,* Appendix, pp. 48, 53, or *Schiele,* pp. 171, 179.

[11] *Dilthey,* Appendix, pp. 51-52ff., or *Schiele,* pp. 177ff. This idea too (cf. above p. 117 and note) suggests Aristotelean influence.

and not in some outside principle or power. This point is fixed and remains fixed for Schleiermacher.[12]

Another partially extant manuscript, dating from the same period 1789-1792, *Über die Freiheit*, criticizes the Kantian postulate of freedom. Schleiermacher begins by putting this question: "How must the activity of the faculty of desire be constituted if it is to be compatible with the recognition of moral responsibility?"[13] His answer is threefold: (1) there must be a "moral impulse" of some sort, (2) this moral impulse must have an equal chance with every other impulse to become the determining factor in action, and (3) the cause which makes this impulse determining in a particular action must lie within the self, not outside of it. That is, in cases of moral responsibility, this cause must lie "within the totality of present impressions," or within the state of soul which can be brought about by the course of these impressions.[14] Examining these three conditions, Schleiermacher concludes that moral responsibility is compatible with determination by immanent motives, and thinks it unnecessary to postulate a "transcendental freedom" for the sake of morality.[15]

About this time Schleiermacher, like many other German intellectuals, became interested in Spinoza, the reputed philosophical villain of preceding years. Because he found much to approve in Spinoza's phil-

---

[12] Cf. above p. 20 and note on the same page. See also *Schiele*, pp. 177ff.
[13] *Dilthey*, Appendix, p. 24.
[14] *Dilthey*, Appendix, pp. 26-27.
[15] *Dilthey*, Appendix, pp. 28-46. An essay by W. Loew, *Das Grundproblem der Ethik Schleiermacher's in seiner Beziehung zu Kant's Ethik* discusses the issue between Schleiermacher and Kant on this point very thoroughly.

osophy, because of his strictures on Kant's theory of freedom, because of his monistic inclinations generally, and his emphasis, in contrast to Fichte, on man's sense of "absolute dependence," it has been customary to call Schleiermacher a determinist.[16] And yet his *Soliloquies* (*Monologen*) are from beginning to end a glorification of the freedom which he claims to have found. The truth, of course, is that Schleiermacher's philosophy can be identified neither with the position of Kant, nor of Spinoza; it is a composite structure of its own, embracing many diverse elements. Like Hegel, Schleiermacher believed that "whoever would master philosophy must understand its history,"[17] and through historical study he became sensitive to many different considerations and provided himself with very varied intellectual resources. What he borrowed from Kant and Spinoza he modified and wove finely together with other ideas into a new pattern.

Schleiermacher's first Spinoza studies apparently date from about 1792. Cradled, as he had been, in pietist devotion, but now uncertain in his conceptions of God and man, he was deeply impressed by Spinoza's idea of substance, and by the justice which it did to one side of religious consciousness, namely our sense of dependence on the infinite whole of things. Spinoza's conception of universal order also satisfied his sense of scientific system. But there seemed to be a misanthropical element in Spinozism, belittling human

[16] See, for example, Ueberweg's *History of Philosophy*.
In regard to the sense of "absolute dependence," cf. pp. 154-155.

[17] *Werke*, III, v. 4¹, p. 15. Schleiermacher's chief studies in the history of philosophy are to be found in *Werke*, III, vols. 1, 2, 3, and 4¹, those in the history of Christianity in *Werke* I, vols. 2, 6, 7, 8, 11. See also *Letters*, v. 1, p. 14.

passion, will, and personality. To be an individual, of any species whatsoever, means in the Spinozistic metaphysics to be limited; a human being is a small fragment of nature, transcending pettiness only through intellectual comprehension of universal order. Kantian philosophy, on the other hand, while granting that human nature is radically limited, nevertheless recognizes an absolute dignity in man's moral will. It respects not only the natural order which intelligence strives to comprehend, but still more the moral order which will strives to create. Moreover, if Spinozism with its consistent intellectualism more fully honors the rational form of truth, Kantianism in its critical, agnostic aspect shows greater regard for the empirical element in science. Schleiermacher's thought moved in both philosophies.

As early as 1793 he seems to have entertained the possibility of combining their strong points; at least, so it would appear from his commentary on Spinoza, *Kurze Darstellung des Spinozistischen Systems,* to which Dilthey assigns that date.[18] This essay, like Herder's *Gott* (1787) and Jakobi's more famous *Briefe über die Lehre des Spinoza* (1785), shows how the attempt to determine what the hitherto maligned and neglected Spinoza really stood for, combined with other intellectual forces present in Germany at the end of the eighteenth century to produce a new philosophic tradition. Schleiermacher notes that Kant and Spinoza both distinguish between existence *per se* and exis-

[18] *Dilthey,* Appendix, p. 64ff., and also *Dilthey,* pp. 147-152. For a full text of the essay see *Werke,* III, v. 4¹, pp. 283-311. The essay also compares Spinoza's philosophy with that of Leibniz, but it is significant that the real issues are felt to be those between Spinoza and Kant. Cf. p. xxxii above.

tence *per aliud*. According to Spinoza only one infinite being can exist *per se*, for finite being is limited, and the limit must be *per aliud*. Kant approaches and handles the distinction somewhat differently. He declines to characterize being *an sich* in any way, since all existence that we can know is, by the very fact of its being known, finite and *per aliud*. Schleiermacher tries to show that these two positions, Kant's and Spinoza's, are not as far apart as they appear. Kant, while agnostic with respect to existence *per se*, moves in Spinoza's direction, Schleiermacher thinks, when, in treating the antinomies of reason, he identifies noumenal being with the Unconditioned. To be sure, this Kantian Unconditioned can not be called one or "positively infinite" without dogmatism. Being as such is pure existence in reference to which both Leibnitzean pluralism and Spinozistic monism must be transcended. Herein Schleiermacher agrees with Kant. He believes, however, that Spinoza himself approaches this critical, agnostic position, when he affirms that substance has an infinite number of attributes, only two of which are revealed to our intellect. With respect to existence *per aliud*, Schleiermacher thinks it possible to unite Spinoza's account with Kant's in some such terms as these: "The finite beings which man knows are an appearance that the modes of substance's attributes produce through the infinitely diverse combinations of their parts."[19] It would seem from this proposition that Schleiermacher is trying to say: Yes, Kant is right in holding our experience to be a very finite, particularly conditioned, phenomenal affair, but at the same time it is possible to believe that this expe-

[19] *Werke*, III, v. 4^1, p. 301.

ri nce is part of an imposing system of absolute order and being, such as Spinoza describes.

Besides the essay just considered, there is an unpublished manuscript of Schleiermacher's entitled *Spinozismus*, in which the important question is raised as to the ultimate ground of individuality, the *principium individui*. Schleiermacher endeavors to distinguish between substantiality and individuality, and denies that Leibniz's metaphysics of plural substances (monads) explains individuality any better than Spinoza's monistic view of substance. At the same time he confesses that in this "crucial problem (*Kernpunkt*) of philosophic theory," he himself does not know "where to cast anchor."[20]

Sec. 2. *Years of Insight* (1792-1802).

To recapitulate the foregoing: Schleiermacher in his earliest writings traces out for himself certain abstract relationships. The "moral law" is a formula for attaining the "highest good" (*Über das höchste Gut* 1789). The "highest good" is the harmonious development of man's various faculties (*Über den Wert des Lebens*, 1793). Moral responsibility does not necessitate transcendental freedom (*Über die Freiheit* 1792). Existence *per se* is infinite being, and hence unknowable, but phenomena exist in and through it (*Kurze Darstellung des Spinozistischen Systems* 1793). Substantiality does not explain individuality (*Spinozismus* 1793-'94).

The way a youthful mind will pursue a suggestion of reason in tenuous abstractions like these is uncanny. Still more inscrutable, however, is the way in which

[20] See *Dilthey*, p. 151, and *Dilthey*, Appendix, pp. 68-69.

such an abstract scheme, when it has once engaged the mind, serves both to promote and to obstruct, to clarify and to obscure whatever fresh and original experience the world has in store for the individual. In Schleiermacher's case the experience and ideas, which in his maturity he recognized as his most original and highest insights, were not clearly implicated in the web of his earliest speculations, but came to him independently as the spiritual deposit of a richer life in the years 1792 to 1802. "The sublime revelation came from within; it was not produced by any code of ethics or system of philosophy."[21] Yet who can define what latent effect the early speculations had in eliciting from this richer life its cardinal revelations? Certainly the new web of ideas, which Schleiermacher wove in the light of these revelations, also has in it a pattern based on his earlier ideas.

More specifically, Schleiermacher's philosophical development appears to have taken about the following course. Both at Schlobitten, where he lived in the home of the Dohna family, and at Berlin in the romantic circle, he saw attractive forms of human life concretely realized. He "saw clearly that each man is meant to represent humanity in his own way, combining its elements uniquely."[22] In previous years he had abstractly defined the "highest good" as the harmonious development of human faculties. Now, without changing the definition, he began to identify this "good" with concrete forms of development such as he saw. "Freedom," defined previously as determination by a moral impulse, he now began to identify,

[21] See above p. 29.
[22] See above p. 31. Also pp. xxxviiff.

quite consistently, with the imprint of human character upon nature, and in a heightened sense with the imprint of individualized human character.[23] To divine individual character, and to live so as to enhance it, seemed to him more and more the essence of morality. In self-knowledge and in knowledge of other selves was to be found that ideal sense of life, which preserved the image of good entire, instead of opening, like Kantian ethics, an everlasting breach between the disparate goods of sense and reason.

This increased regard for individual character as a pivotal fact in the moral order brought Schleiermacher back to the question raised in his study of Spinoza: what is the status of individuality in the universal order? In that hybrid of Spinozistic-Kantian metaphysics, which he had conceived in 1793, individuality was held to be different from substantiality, but no conclusion was reached as to its nature and ground.[24] Nor was Schleiermacher to reach a definite conclusion in this matter for many years. It is not difficult to understand why, when one considers the many aspects of the problem as he saw it. For him, almost all philosophic issues began to center on this *Kernpunkt*. In the first place, Spinoza and Kant, indeed virtually the whole philosophic tradition, taught him to identify reason with the universal, but he himself was coming more and more to identify a large part of moral reason, at least, with respect for individuality. At the same time, while it was largely moral experience that interested him in individuality, he was unwilling to make moral qualities the criterion of all individuality.

[23] See above pp. 28-33.
[24] See above p. 123.

Furthermore, he had not in the least lost his religious feeling for the infinite "whole that stands over against man,"[25] so that he did not think of all value as associated with the individual and the unique. Again, he was still a Kantian, in his agnosticism with respect to absolute substance, in his view that knowledge reveals only a manifold of interrelated phenomena. And, finally, he was just beginning to realize that his earlier attempt to combine Spinozistic and Kantian ideas had been made half-blindly, without critically facing the question of what after all should determine the structure of a philosophic system. His was not a mind to cut these Gordian knots by some single blow. It took him many years to collect the group of concepts by which he finally tried to express his view of the place of individuality in the universal order.[26]

Meanwhile, however, he was riding on the magic carpet of his own immediate experiences, "in that beautiful time of my life (1792-1800), when I came into contact with so much that was new."[27] The golden tree of life abundantly provided fruitful insights without demanding that they fall at once into a complete theoretic system. Moreover, Schleiermacher was justified in believing that these new insights of his into individual moral and religious consciousness were not without their significance for philosophic theory. However, he might finally describe the relations between individual and universe when he had attained philosophic clarity, whether in terms that could somehow be assimilated to the older speculative traditions or not, he knew that in any case his own more recent in-

[25] *On Religion*, p. 37.
[26] See below p. 137-141.
[27] See above p. 41. Parenthesis and dates mine.

sights were not adequately expressed in the ideas of Spinoza, or of Kant, or indeed of any philosopher with whom he was acquainted.

This was the point in his philosophical development that Schleiermacher had reached when, under the encouragement of Schlegel and other friends, he wrote the *Speeches on Religion* (1799), a work which expressly precludes all attempts to define the universe and the individual, or to penetrate to the roots of their relationship, but which dwells at length upon religion, defined as a sense which the individual has for the universe. The notable characteristic of religious consciousness, thinks Schleiermacher, is the way in which "love" for the universe and "love" for the individual are fused in it. In scientific consciousness the individual attains a universal viewpoint, but effaces his particularity. In moral consciousness some interest of human will, be it individual or collective, is favored above other being. But religion exhibits the individual, steeping the universe in his own uniqueness, concerned to find his own particular being in communion with the all.[28] This power of individual mind to universalize even its individuality finds no recognition in the metaphysics of Spinoza or of Kant, for whom universality and individuality remain antithetic. In their view the individual transcends his individuality when he rises either to an intellectual comprehension of the

---

[28] Cf. pp. xlviii-l. Unfortunately we are not able to trace the steps by which Schleiermacher reached these views of religious consciousness as well as we can trace the development of other ideas in his philosophy. An emphasis on the emotional, in contrast to the dogmatic, side of religion must have been present from the start in his pietistic upbringing, but whether he made this central and how he interpreted it in the period before 1796 we do not know. See pp. xviii, 117-118.

one universal order, or to devotion to the essential moral law. But Schleiermacher would emphasize a type of experience in which there is productive, inner continuity between the individual and the universal.[29]

Like the *Speeches on Religion*, the *Soliloquies*, published a few months later, aim to describe Schleiermacher's new experiences and insights, in this case particularly his insights into moral consciousness, without, however, striving for close definition, or for a dialectical treatment of concepts, in short, without determining precisely what these experiences might yield for a comprehensive system of philosophic thought. The lavish use of the term *Geist* (spirit) in the *Soliloquies* is itself indicative of this fact, a term rich in moral and religious connotations through popular usage, but of unstable scientific value until Schelling, Hegel, and Schleiermacher made an attempt to stabilize its meaning some years later (c. 1810). For the most part, the *Soliloquies* depict things as refracted in a certain kind of moral and esthetic consciousness; the author reviews his development from the standpoint of the ideal he has reached. Thus, for example, he retrospects upon his point of view before he had discovered the significance of individuality, and emphasizes chiefly the moral implications of that former position. "For a long time I too was content with the discovery of a universal reason; I worshipped the one essential being as the highest, and so believed that there is but a single right way of acting in every situ-

[29] *On Religion*, pp. 43, 58, 228. The foreshadowing of the Hegelian metaphysics of being in this description of religious consciousness is unmistakeable. Schleiermacher's later thought in fact moved in the direction of such a metaphysics, with important qualifications, as we shall see below, pp. 137-141.

ation, that the conduct of all men should be alike, each differing from the other only by reason of his place and station in the world. I thought humanity revealed itself as varied only in the manifold diversity of outward acts, that man himself, the individual, was not a being uniquely fashioned, but of one substance and everywhere the same."[30] The criticism in this passage is moral, and need not imply a precise metaphysics.

But there are certain passages in the *Soliloquies,* as written in 1800, which sound as if Schleiermacher, under the inspiration of his new insights, were abandoning the "critical" position, to swing himself with great élan into a dogmatic idealistic metaphysics of a sort that affirms the universe to be fundamentally an infinite community of spiritual individuals. Of course, his enthusiasm in the *Soliloquies* for this point of view should be regarded as thoroughly genuine, but nevertheless as enthusiasm for a point of view in the atmosphere of which he was living, and not as the exposition of his philosophical system. Schleiermacher had not developed a system of philosophy when he wrote the *Soliloquies,* and when he did so in later years, it was not in accord with these extremely "idealistic" passages. He himself recognized this so completely that he changed many of the passages in question as early as 1810, when a second edition of the text was published.[31] In the light of these changes, it seems

[30] See p. 30 above. The period of life referred to in this passage is that before 1793 or thereabouts. See p. xxxiiiff.

[31] Cf. passages of the text on pp. 16-17, with the subsequent modifications as given in the notes on pp. 104-105. Cf. also below pp. 134-142 for the later system. I now turn to describe that system without commenting further on the viewpoint of the *Speeches* or the *Soliloquies* as this has been done in the Introduction.

as if Schleiermacher in 1800 had to a certain extent clothed his thought in a current metaphysical idiom, which he soon realized was an unnecessarily and unjustifiably extravagant way of putting the essential facts he had discovered about individuality and moral consciousness.

Sec. 3. *The System-Making of Later Years* (1802-1834).

There are thirty-one volumes in the complete edition of Schleiermacher's works,[32] but only four of these were written with an immediate view to publication. Ten of them are collections of his sermons, two of public and professional addresses, while thirteen were posthumously pieced together out of lecture notes. Two more, though prepared for the press by Schleiermacher himself (*Der christliche Glaube*, 1821-'22), contain material that was first used in lectures. Thus, by far the larger portion of his work was produced under a predominantly didactic, rather than a literary impulse. Schleiermacher says that he realized his essentially didactic bent early in life, but that he never discovered any talent for writing. A year after leaving the university he wrote to a friend: "I have fully given up the thought of writing, because I am certain that I should never be able to accomplish anything in that line."[33] He rarely, if ever wrote out his sermons before delivering them. It was the influence of Friedrich Schlegel and other literary friends, with whom

[32] Published by G. Reimer, Berlin, 1835-'64. In addition to these thirty-one, there are five volumes of letters also published by Reimer, and five volumes of Plato's dialogues translated by Schleiermacher into German, Berlin, 1804-1810.

[33] *Briefe*, v. 4, p. 42.

he kept company in Berlin, that led him for a time into literary channels,[34] but even as an author he chose to imagine himself in the situation of a speaker, or, in one case, of a correspondent: he wrote "Speeches on Religion," "Soliloquies," a dialogue called "Christmas Eve" (*Weihnachtsfeier*), and the "Confidential Letters" about Schlegel's *Lucinde*.

Schleiermacher's literary élan spent itself in these four works, all of them written between 1798 and 1806, the years when he was closest to the "romantic circle." What he did before and after this period has a severely academic cast, scholarly researches of an exegetical or historical kind, logical analyses of technical philosophical concepts, and attempts at the systematic presentation of various subject-matters, e. g., "dialectic," ethics, psychology, pedagogy, politics, esthetics, dogmatics, Christian history, history of philosophy, and hermeneutics. Only in his preaching did Schleiermacher throughout life keep in contact with a general audience. His academic career began in 1804 when he was appointed professor and chaplain at his own university of Halle, was interrupted by the Napoleonic wars in 1806, and recontinued at the new university of Berlin in 1810, where he remained throughout the rest of his life.

But even before his appointment at Halle, namely in 1802 when the Berlin romantic group was scattered and Schleiermacher went into a kind of exile at Stolpe, his scholarly interests came to the fore.[35] Cut off from his literary friends, he devoted himself, not to the project, hinted at in the *Soliloquies*, of expressing his

[34] See above p. xxxix.
[35] See above p. liv.

outlook on life in a novel,[36] but to the completion of the translation of Plato's dialogues, which he had begun with Schlegel. And he took up again his original plan, for which the *Soliloquies* had been substituted in 1800, of writing a formal critique of Kantian-Fichtean ethics.[37] As he worked on it at Stolpe in the years 1802-'03, simultaneously with the translation of Plato and other historical studies, the project grew into something more comprehensive, *Outlines of a Critique of Previous Ethical Theory*.[38]

This *Critique* is polemic and critical in nature from beginning to end, Schleiermacher's own ethical ideal appearing only indirectly.[39] And for the most part the criticism is formal, that is, it proceeds from the proposition that ethical teaching should form a thoroughly integrated system. Scientific precision and verification are associated with systematic formulation. Now, to say that ethics must be a system means, for Schleiermacher, that each item of ethical teaching, each duty, each virtue, and each good must be defined in the light of all the others, so as not to conflict with them or render them ambiguous, but rather so as to supplement them by clarifying and developing the same idea (perhaps Idea) which they express. What ethics seeks to portray should "be regarded as a complete whole, the parts of which can be understood only in and through the whole."[40]

[36] See above p. xl, 88.

[37] See above p. xl.

[38] Published in *Werke*, III, v. 1, pp. 1-344, and separately in the *Philosophische Bibliothek*, Leipzig, 1908.

[39] See *Werke*, III, v. 1, p. 3ff.

[40] *Werke*, III, v. 1, p. 246. Cf. pp. xix-xxi above with respect to this idea of "system" in Schleiermacher's thought. It also appears at times in the "unsystematically" written *Soliloquies* (see, for instance, pp. 71-72).

APPENDIX 133

Schleiermacher finds, however, that historically the philosophers have not developed their ethical teachings in this thoroughly systematic fashion, and he shows that in consequence the counsels of every known ethical theory are ambiguous. The specific causes of ambiguity are many, for the various philosophers are unsystematic in different respects. For example, there are some who describe the good as consisting of multiple elements without organizing these elements in any hierarchy, or without stating any principle by which a decision can be made between them.[41] Then there are others who begin with some single organizing principle, but who later find it does not accomplish all that they desire. In this predicament a second supplementary principle is frequently introduced, but without explanation of its relations to the first principle.[42] This again gives rise to heteronomy. A very common source of ambiguity lies in the fact that the three aspects of ethical reality, i. e., virtue, duty and good, are treated separately according to unrelated principles. The virtues recommended would often not lead to the fulfillment of the duties enjoined, nor the latter to the realization of the goods desired.[43] It is a leading principle of Schleiermacher's in this regard that virtues, duties, and goods are related as efficient, formal, and final causes of the same ethical process.[44]

Schleiermacher believes that, all things considered, Plato and Spinoza among the classic philosophers have avoided these various pitfalls best. Plato's ethics espe-

[41] *Werke*, III, v. 1, pp. 78-92, 141.
[42] *Werke*, III, v. 1, pp. 104-106, 155ff., 208ff.
[43] *Werke*, III, v. 1, pp. 155ff., 126, 190, 196, 215-217, 174-175.
[44] Cf. pp. xxxi-xxxii, 116-117, 147.

cially comes near to being a perfect system, organizing all its parts with reference to the aim of contemplating "the idea of the good."[45] Perhaps Schleiermacher misinterprets Aristotle, whose leading principle he regards as hedonistic with qualifications that result in ambiguities.[46] If the idea of the "prudent man" as determining the good were taken as central, perhaps Aristotle would fare better as a systematic moralist.

Granting Schleiermacher's premise, that ethics must be systematic in his sense, the strictures he passes upon other moral philosophers seem just, though hard. This is no doubt a case where it is comparatively easy to criticize, and the vital question is whether Schleiermacher himself fares better in his own constructive efforts. After receiving his appointment at Halle, he lectured on ethics repeatedly, both there and at Berlin in later years. Moreover, he put some of his leading ideas into a series of addresses on moral philosophy delivered before the Royal Academy of Sciences in the years 1825 to 1830. But he never completed the exposition of his ethical system, so that we can judge of it only by piecing together the contents of various essays and note-books.[47]

In order to understand Schleiermacher's ethical system, we must likewise piece together a similar set of essays and lecture-notes on "dialectic," in which he gradually developed his conception of philosophizing

[45] *Werke*, III, v. 1, pp. 33-36, 106, 110-111, 176.
[46] *Werke*, III, v. 1, pp. 113, 177-180, 225.
[47] This is what Alex. Schweizer did in editing *Werke*, III, v. 5. See his Preface. My references to Schleiermacher's *Ethik* or *Sittenlehre* in the sequel refer to this volume. But comparison should be made with Otto Braun's *Schleiermacher's Entwurf zu einem System der Sittenlehre*, a later editing of the manuscripts dating from 1804-1816. See Braun's Preface, p. xvi.

and of philosophic system-making in general.[48] According to him, "dialectic" or philosophizing is the art of resolving conflicts in thought, of producing *streitfreies Denken*. Philosophy begins in such conflicts and aims to resolve them. Now, by analyzing the nature of these conflicts, we arrive at two fundamental propositions: (1) thought refers beyond itself to being, and (2) thought involves antitheses. The analysis which leads to the first proposition is briefly as follows: conflict between thinking A is b and thinking A is not b is possible only if the thinking in each case refers beyond itself to the same A. Such "conflict implies that an identical object is being considered, and thereby implies a general reference of thought to Being."[49] Schleiermacher is aware that this "reference of thought to being," while apparently implied in the process of thinking, has also been construed as a radical obstacle to the success of thinking. For if thought refers to a transcendent object, how can it be tested? His answer is: it cannot be tested by the comparison of idea and object, except in cases of self-knowledge, where alone we are directly in touch with the object

[48] Cf. above p. xx, 126. Schleiermacher lectured on "dialectic" in 1811, 1814, 1818, 1822, 1828, and 1831. L. Jonas edited the available materials in *Werke*, III, v. 4², and a new critical edition was made by J. Halpern, Berlin, 1903. In my account of Schleiermacher's system I have run the lectures on "dialectic" and on "ethics" together as forming a whole.

[49] *Werke*, III, v. 4², p. 584ff. In the above section, and throughout the *Dialektik*, Schleiermacher is treating primarily of logical thought and of *Wissen*. But the most general characteristics of such thought seem to him to hold also of practical and esthetic *thinking*, and hence I have used the generic term. Cf. p. 142 and note.

of thought.[50] But thought can be tested in a measure by its relation to other thought. If all ideas having a common reference agree with each other, and are consistent with ideas having other references, then at least we should have no reason to suppose a discrepancy between our thought and the object to which it referred, even though we should not be able to perceive or to prove an agreement.[51]

Schleiermacher holds that such agreement among ideas can never be perfect, because of the individualizing tendency that pervades all being.[52] Hence there is no perfectly *streitfreies Denken*, no impeccable scientific knowledge. On the other hand, he finds sufficient intellectual agreement resulting here and there from certain types of inquiry to convince him that there is significant correspondence between the structure of being and the structure of logical thought. He believes that in the concepts and propositions of science, reality effects a partial organization of ideas corresponding to a similar, partial organization of powers and their manifestations, which it effects among objects.[53]

[50] *Werke*, III, v. 4², p. 53. This theory, that in self-consciousness thought and its object are in immediate rapport, Schleiermacher shares with many of his contemporaries, notably Fichte and Schopenhauer. Unlike these two idealists, however, he does not base an idealistic metaphysics on this theory, i. e., he does not infer that in self-consciousness we discover what it means to be. See pp. 139-140 below and note.

[51] Schleiermacher apparently does not consider the difficulties which may be involved in the comparison of ideas themselves, difficulties which George Santayana has driven home so effectively in his *Scepticism and Animal Faith*.

[52] Cf. pp. 137-141 and *Werke*, III, v. 5, pp. 1166120. Even in scientific knowledge, where individualized spirituality yields for the most part to a universal reason, individuality still manifests itself. Schleiermacher gives some interesting examples derived from a comparison of the scientific terminologies and traditions of the different nations. See *Werke*, III, v. 4², p. 577ff.

[53] *Werke*, III, v. 4², pp. 111-146.

To understand more fully how Schleiermacher conceives thought and being, it is necessary to trace the development of that second fundamental proposition, which he discovered in his analysis of logical conflicts: thought involves antitheses.[54] It is the nature and implications of these antitheses which must be examined. The life of thought is everywhere full of distinctions, and seems to be characterized by a double movement, at once toward relating and uniting what is distinct and toward differentiating what is one. The scientist, for example, looks for unity and diversity in the same subject-matter, seeking to discover more and more minute distinctions, but also interpreting them through more and more general facts in which the distinctions seem to be grounded. This double movement gives rise, on the one hand, to the idea of God, as a highest unity embracing all distinctions, and on the other, to the idea of the world, as all distinctions embraced in this unity. God and the world are not to be identified, but "neither can we think of one without the other"; they are correlatives. Both are transcendent; the world transcends all actual thought as a *terminus ad quem* toward which the process of discovery approaches; God transcends thought absolutely as a *terminus a quo*, in which thinking is grounded, but which it cannot approach.[55] At the same time, God and the world are in a sense immanent, i. e., they are represented in human experience, in a sense which is to be explained later. (See below, p. 140ff.)

To say that thought involves antitheses, however, is

[54] See p. 135 above.
[55] *Werke*, III, v. 4^2, pp. 154-172.

to say more than that it involves distinctions. An antithesis is a special kind of distinction, in which one member somehow involves its opposite, e. g., hot and cold, wet and dry, hard and soft, etc. To say that thought involves such distinctions is to indicate a certain relativism in experience, and a need for qualified statement.[56] Experience exhibits a mixture of opposites. Now, hot and cold, hard and soft, etc., are antitheses which appear in some experiences, but not in others; they are not universal. Schleiermacher, however, describes a group of antitheses which he believes are universal, involved in the very nature of thought and its objects. Each antithesis in this group appears in various forms, so that more than one pair of terms exists to characterize it. Thus, one of these universal antitheses is that between the organic and the intellectual, between what Kant called "matter" and "form," between a sense-manifold spacially and temporally organized, on the one hand, and a system of meanings, on the other. A second is that between the universal and the particular, the general and the individual, the common and the unique. Embracing these two antitheses within itself, there is what Schleiermacher calls the "highest antithesis," namely that between "thing" and "spirit," the known and the knowing, the real and the ideal, nature and reason. This highest antithesis embraces the other two inasmuch as whatever is *predominantly* natural, real, and "thinglike" is *predominantly* organic, material, spacial and temporal, made up of particulars or individuals, and abounding in uniqueness, whereas whatever is *predominantly* reasonable, ideal, and spiritual is *predominantly* intellectual, for-

[56] *Werke*, III, v. 5, p. 15.

mal, meaningful, of a general, common, and universal character.[57]

The italicizing of the word *predominantly* in the foregoing statement points to a significant characteristic of the antitheses in thought, which must be examined next. An antithesis in which there was a perfect equilibrium of forces, i. e., in which each member cancelled the effect of the other by working in an opposite direction to an equal degree, such an antithesis would frustrate thought. That which is equally organic and intellectual, universal and particular (active and passive), in the same respect, cannot be thought any more than can the purely intellectual and universal, or the purely organic and particular. Every thought and every object of thought must be both intellectual and organic, universal and particular, *and it must be predominantly one in some respects and predominantly the other in other respects.*[58] Hence that which is natural and real is not only predominantly natural and real, but in some respects predominantly reasonable and ideal, and likewise what is real and ideal is nevertheless in some respects predominantly natural and real.

Points of similarity between this aspect of Schleier-

[57] *Werke*, III, v. 5, p. 25, and v. 4^2, pp. 76ff. "Der höchste Gegensaz, unter dem uns alle andern begriffen vorschweben, ist der des dinglichen und des geistigen Seins." For the other two universal antitheses, embraced in this highest one, see respectively *Werke*, III, v. 4^2, pp. 55ff., 111ff., and v. 5, pp. 103-116, 116-120. Another general antithesis closely related to these in Schleiermacher's thought is that between the active and the passive, will and compulsion, the ethical and the physical. See *Werke*, III, v. 4^2, pp. 147-150, and cf. below pp. 141ff.

[58] *Werke*, III, v. 5, p. 21. "Jeder Gegensaz, also, in wiefern er in einem bestimmten Sein und Wissen gegeben ist, muss gegeben sein in der Zwiefaltigkeit des Uebergewichts hier seines einen, dort seines andern Gliedes."

macher's "dialectic" and Hegelian dialectic are not far to seek. Unlike Hegel, however, Schleiermacher did not affirm his dialectic of thought to be identical with the metaphysics of being. He found sufficient evidence to "incline" him toward the view that there is significant correspondence between the two, but he did not believe the correspondence to be complete, and he allowed the possibility of other inclinations being equally justified.[59] In brief, Schleiermacher remained from beginning to end a Kantian in his belief that we know only in part. Hence, according to him, every attempt to state what are the most general and fundamental truths involves, not only analysis, but also inclination, i. e., *Gesinnung*.[60] His own inclination, as he himself interprets it, is to look for the most general and fundamental truths "in our own being," since that is the most complicated being of which we know. As far as we know, more different kinds of activity are organized in us, more antitheses are brought together in man than anywhere else. Among others, "the highest antithesis will also be found in our being (for our being . . . is determined by all antitheses), and since it is more immediately present to us than any other being, we should look for this antithesis here." This is as near as Schleiermacher comes to metaphysical idealism.[61] The way in which man endeavors progressively to harmonize the contrasts in his experience gives us the best suggestion we have of God and the world. Man strives to see more of the universal in the particular, and more of the particular in the universal. He

[59] Cf. pp. xx, 135-136.
[60] *Werke*, III, v. 4^2, p. 76.
[61] *Werke*, III, v. 5, p. 25. There is a very characteristic blend of scholastic and of subjective idealism in this reasoning.

strives to make the ideal more and more real, and the real more and more ideal. He strives to have everything in time and space full of meaning, and to give everything meaningful a local habitation and a name. Coupled with this human striving is a belief in its connection with reality, a conviction that the ground or basis for ideal experience already exists, that man is not seeking a mirage, but the actual, a reality as yet known only in part. He believes that if he knew fully, he should know God, a being in whom the real is ideal, whose only compulsion is his own action, but whose action is necessary, for whom no material is meaningless and no thought empty, who is at once the only being absolutely universal and absolutely individual.

This idea of God, which in cognitive experience is purely formal, is enriched in religious experience by our "feeling for the universe" and the consequent treatment which imagination gives to it. Moral experience likewise requires this idea of God, not as an image of the moral ideal, but as implying that tie between the intellectual and the volitional which is essential to morality.[62] Schleiermacher's lectures on *Dialektik* deal primarily with cognitive experience, but towards the end of Part I (as arranged by Jonas) these and other points are made regarding religious and moral experience to show that these latter realms of experience exhibit the same fundamental features and antitheses which thought discovers in its cognitive employment. Schleiermacher's conception, in this mat-

[62] *Werke*, III, v. 4², pp. 147-154. Cf. *Soliloquies*, p. 28. This is an interesting modification of Kant's theory that God is required to connect the rational and sensible worlds, an idea which Schleiermacher rejected from the first. See p. 117.

ter, is that while science or theory (i. e., *Wissenschaft*) is by no means the only type of experience and thought, the other types seem to run their courses *within* the same general, dialectical order revealed by science.[63] It is a mistake to think that his philosophy of religion involves the idea of a "double-truth," so that what is true in science could be false in theology, and vice versa.[64]

The universal relevance of "dialectic" to all parts of experience is well illustrated in Schleiermacher's classification of the sciences. According to him, there are four fundamental sciences, Natural History, Physics, History, and Ethics (*Naturkunde, Physik, Geschichtskunde, Ethik*).[65] This classification is based on a cross-division, using as one basis the antithesis between nature and reason, and for the other basis the antithesis between the empirical and the intellectual. Natural History and Physics are sciences which study predominantly natural being, while History and Ethics study predominantly reasonable being. Natural History and History are predominantly empirical, i. e., concerned with the collection of particular facts; Physics and Ethics are predominantly intellectual, i. e., concerned

[63] Because of this consonance I have used the generic term "thought" in my account of Schleiermacher's "dialectic" (see p. 135 and note) without drawing the distinctions between esthetic, practical, and theoretic thought which he draws in his own *Einleitung* (see *Werke*, III, v. 4², pp. 568-577).

[64] It has been argued that Schleiermacher's reference to a religious sense of "absolute dependence" implies that religious feeling transcends cognitive experience, in which we discover only conditional and not absolute dependence. But Schleiermacher appears to deny this interpretation of his theory of religious emotion expressly in the second edition of the *Soliloquies* (see above p. 105). The sense of absolute dependence does not reveal absolute dependence. Cf. also below pp. 154, 163.

[65] *Werke*, III, v. 5, pp. 32-37.

with the discovery of general principles. Thus:

1. Natural History is the empirical observation of all existences in being which is predominantly natural.
2. Physics is the intellectual study of principles or essences in being which is predominantly natural.
3. History is the empirical observation of all existences in being which is predominantly reasonable.
4. Ethics is the intellectual study of principles or essences in being which is predominantly reasonable.[66]

It must be remembered, however, in interpreting the above, that according to Schleiermacher's analysis of thought and experience, every item of experience is predominantly characterized by one member of a fundamental antithesis in some respects and by the opposite member in other respects. As a consequence there is no subject-matter that belongs to any one of these sciences to the exclusion of the rest. All being is in some respects the subject-matter of physics, in others of ethics, in some of natural history, in others of history. And hence, Schleiermacher adds that none of these four sciences can be perfected without a like perfection of all the others. "The science of ethics is at no time further advanced than the science of physics," and vice versa; both are in like manner mutually dependent upon history and natural history.[67]

Schleiermacher's belief in the fundamental unity of scientific theory and method, throughout realms frequently contrasted, such as physics and ethics for in-

[66] *Werke*, III, v. 5, pp. 34ff.'
[67] *Werke*, III, v. 5, pp. 42ff.

stance, is further illustrated by his view that moral law is analogous to natural law. In an address delivered before the Royal Academy of Sciences in 1825 on *Naturgesetz und Sittengesetz* he criticizes the position that natural laws describe the way in which things invariably do behave, while moral laws state the way in which they ought to behave.[68] On the contrary, says Schleiermacher, both natural and moral laws are statements of the way in which things do behave, and also of the way in which they ought to behave, if the things are beings conforming to the definitions of the laws. Natural and moral laws differ only in defining and treating of different kinds of beings. Moral beings conform to moral laws as invariably as do natural beings to natural laws, and the latter ought to conform to natural laws as truly as the former ought to conform to the moral. Furthermore, deviations occur from natural laws as well as from moral. Some of these deviations indicate that all laws, natural and moral, are but approximate generalizations. Others indicate, however, that every being stands under a multiplicity of laws, and that its conformity to one law, natural or moral, is conditioned by its conformity to others. Only as conditioned by other than moral laws does a being do evil, and hence "the antithesis between good and bad falls outside the description of ethics," which deals only with *predominantly* moral or reasonable being.[69] Again, since Schleiermacher defines freedom as self-development, and morality as the self-development of a moral being, it follows that only as condi-

[68] *Werke*, III, v. 2, pp. 397-418. Cf. also *Werke*, III, v. 5, pp. 38ff.

[69] *Werke*, III, v. 5, pp. 52-53. "Der Gegensaz von gut und böse fällt ausser der Sittenlehre."

tioned by other than moral laws is a being brought under compulsion. "The antithesis between freedom and necessity likewise falls outside the description of ethics."[70] Of course, there is nothing in these principles to preclude the possibility of a being developing from one kind of being into another kind of being. A natural being conforms to natural laws, and a moral being to moral laws, but some of these laws may be such that the natural being develops into a moral being. Finally, it is important in this connection to recall that, according to the principles of Schleiermacher's "dialectic," we should not expect to find any being predominantly natural or moral in all respects, but rather predominantly the one in some respects, and the other in others.

Ethics, then, is a descriptive science, descriptive of the essences, the laws, and the principles to which being conforms in so far as it is predominantly reasonable. In outlining the formal structure of this science Schleiermacher adheres to his view that ethical reality manifests itself in the three modes of good, duty, and virtue (related as final, formal, and efficient causes of the same process.)[71] The fundamental mode, however, is that of the good, and this is now defined, in terms of the "highest antithesis" disclosed in the "dialectic," as a predominantly reasonable interpenetration of nature and reason.[72] It will be recalled that both nature and reason, as defined in the "dialectic," are rich in qualities, and hence their interpenetration will

[70] *Werke*, III, v. 5, pp. 63-64. "Der Gegensaz von Freiheit und Nothwendigkeit fällt ausser der Sittenlehre."

[71] Cf. pp. 133 above. A separate division of the *Sittenlehre*, as published, is devoted to each of these modes in the order named. *Werke*, III, v. 5, pp. 71-84.

[72] *Werke*, III, v. 5, p. 27, 85-87. Cf. above p. 138.

produce many permutations and combinations, in other words, a richly varied good. This variety, however, will not be a mere medley, but will have a structure, since the many qualities of nature and of reason group themselves around certain major antitheses subsumed under the general antithesis of nature and reason itself.[73] The interpenetration of nature and reason is not the interpenetration of two chaotic manifolds, but the crossing of a predominantly organic manifold with one predominantly intellectual, and of one predominantly individualized with one predominantly universalized. As a result of this crossing, the realm of the good comes to have four great provinces: (1) a province in which nature appears predominantly as the organ of a chiefly universal reason, (2) a province in which it appears predominantly as the organ of a chiefly individualized reason, (3) a province in which it appears predominantly as the intelligible symbol of a chiefly universal reason, and (4) a province in which it appears predominantly as the intelligible symbol of a chiefly individualized reason. This description of ethical being as characterized by nature's becoming the organ and sign of both universal and individual reason was amply foreshadowed in the *Soliloquies* of 1800.[74] Here in Schleiermacher's later thought the idea is worked out more systematically, and finally, the abstractions are linked up definitely with concrete realms of life: the first province with the realm of commerce (*Verkehr*) and its regulation by the state, the second with the realm of personal assets (*Eigenthum*), their enjoyment and enhancement in fellowships, the third

[73] See above p. 138.
[74] See above pp. 19-20, and cf. *Werke*, III, v. 5, pp. 88-96.

with the realm of science (*Wissen*) and its pursuit in schools, and the fourth with the realm of religion (*Gefühl*) and its cultivation in churches.[75]

Schleiermacher's delineation of the domain of ethical being with its four provinces can be presented at a glance in the following diagram:

ORGANIC

	Commerce (*Verkehr*)	Personal Assets (*Eigenthum*)	
UNIVERSAL	Nature the organ of a universal reason.	Nature the organ of an individual reason.	INDIVIDUAL
	The State	Fellowships	
	Science (*Wissen*)	Religion (*Gefühl*)	
	Nature the intelligible symbol of a universal reason.	Nature the intelligible symbol of an individual reason.	
	Schools	Churches	

INTELLECTUAL

This conception of the good controls Schleiermacher's treatment of duties and virtues in the second and third parts respectively of his *Sittenlehre*, quite in accordance with his theory as to the three modes of ethical reality and their relationships. Each province of ethical being has its duties, virtues, and goods, determined alike by the fundamental character of that province. Thus, for example, in the field of commerce and of the state, the first duty is: "Enter into every association in such a way that your entrance amounts to an assimilation."[76] The second duty in the same field is: "Enter into every association in such a way as to retain your

[75] *Werke*, III, v. 5, pp. 120ff.
[76] *Werke*, III, v. 5, p. 439.

entire individuality."[77] It is not difficult to infer from these typical propositions that Schleiermacher is still grappling in the ethical system of his later years with that fundamental problem, which as early as 1794 he took to be the *Kernpunkt* of philosophical theory, how to do justice at once to the individual and to the surrounding whole.[78]

To sum up: Schleiermacher's ethical system is determined on the formal side by three major factors, (1) his conception of the relation between goods, duties, and virtues, (2) his view of the major antitheses involved in ethics, and (3) his delineation of the four provinces of ethical being. The first of these goes back to the earliest days of his philosophizing, the second and third largely to the years of his fundamental insights, but with amplifications and systematization occurring in the later years. On the side of content, the system likewise contains much that was present in the *Speeches on Religion* and in the *Soliloquies*. The most significant material addition of the later years is the greater recognition accorded to institutional and social ethics, to the place of the state and the school especially. These later years, it should be remembered, saw the rise of Hegelianism and a general coming to the fore of political and social issues in Germany.[79] Unlike Hegel, however, Schleiermacher assigned, in his later as in his earlier years, a large sphere of the good to predominantly individual reason. How typical of German liberal thought (how unlike British liberalism) is his antithesis between "commerce" as a field for state regulation and a realm of

[77] *Werke*, III, v. 5, p. 445.
[78] See above p. xxxii, 123.
[79] See above pp. lvi-lvii.

personal assets, private goods, to be enjoyed and furthered in free fellowship! How typical of German conditions, again, of the organized intellectualism there prevailing, is his association of schools and academies with the pursuit of science! Behind the highly abstract concepts of Schleiermacher's *Dialektik* and *Sittenlehre* (and the reader can have no conception, even from the foregoing account, how unalleviated their abstraction is!) appears the unmistakable image of concrete forms of life with which he was in such active contact.[80]

II

SCHLEIERMACHER'S CONCEPTION OF A PHILOSOPHER PRIEST

Schleiermacher's position after 1810 as a teacher, a member of the government, and a prominent ecclesiast gave him personal experience in the various provinces of ethics distinguished in his *Sittenlehre*: the state, the school, the church, and fellowships. A witness to his own principle that human development requires "an intimate and necessary tie between practice and theory," he subjected each of these realms to theoretic analysis. In 1817 and 1829 he lectured on politics, in 1813, 1820, and 1826 on pedagogy.[81] But the

[80] In the latter portions of the *Sittenlehre* (*Werke*, III, v. 5, pp. 172-327), where Schleiermacher discusses the realms of commerce, fellowship, science, and religion in more detail, the incidence of his thought on concrete facts is still more apparent.

[81] See *Werke*, III, v. 8 for the materials on politics as edited by Brandis, and v. 9 for those on pedagogy as edited by Platz.

field in which his practical experience was greatest, and where his theory proved most fruitful, was certainly that of religion and the church.

The basis of his thought in this field was laid before 1799, when in his *Speeches on Religion* he conceived religion as essentially an emotional reaction of the individual to the universe.[82] The perfection of his thought in this field came, however, in later years, when as a leader in the religious life of his time, he conceived of the *Kirchenfürst*, a veritable philosopher-priest of the church. The *Kirchenfürst* is one "who attends to the theory and the practice of his church with the highest measure of religious interest and of scientific spirit combined."[83] Of course, he shares the essential feelings of his church, and wishes to see them promoted as an integral part in the good of mankind. But in addition he has a knowledge of the conditions necessary to this end, and thereby weaves the life of his church like a fine thread into the growing texture of society. He mediates his religion to the world, not in a spirit of blind partisanship, but in the spirit of a philosophic knowledge of human good. Thus he becomes the genius of his church, the reason active in its prosperous development.

But where is the *Kirchenfürst* to be found? Like Plato's philosopher-king he is the product of an ideal education. In 1810 the University of Berlin was opened with Schleiermacher as head of the theological faculty. This post of leadership in a new university, inaugurated with so many idealistic hopes, gave him

[82] See pp. xlvii-l.
[83] *Werke*, I, v. 1, p. 8, §9. The section numbers (§) will serve to identify passages in other editions of this text. See Bibliography, p. 168.

APPENDIX 151

the opportunity to propose a program of ecclesiastical education commensurate with his idea of a *Kirchenfürst*. In 1811 he published a *Brief Exposition of Theological Studies*, which outlined the entire field of theological study as he conceived it, but did not develop any portion of that field in detail. Ten years later he published *Der christliche Glaube*, a systematic exposition of dogmatic theology. Taken together these two books show his conception of the *Kirchenfürst's* equipment fairly well.[84]

Theology, according to Schleiermacher, is in the broadest sense identical with that equipment, and has an essentially practical object, which may be defined as the harmonious guidance of a church. "Christian theology is the sum of scientific knowledge and of practical precepts which are necessary for the harmonious guidance of the Christian Church, i. e., without which the ecclesiastical organization of Christianity would be impossible."[85] This association of theology with institutionalized religion is significant. Schleiermacher expressly states that the "Christian faith itself does not need theology in order to take effect in the individual soul or in the family."[86] Theology arises with the church, and only becomes a unified, coherent discipline in relation to the end of church government. Without this end the materials of theology might still exist as parts of other disciplines, such as history and philosophy, but in relation to this end they are united and constitute a positive science. It follows that a

[84] During his professorship at Halle (1804-1806) Schleiermacher had worked over the ground of the theological subjects, and had lectured in them as well as in philosophy.

[85] *Werke*, I, v. 1, pp. 6-7, §5.

[86] *Werke*, I, v. 1, p. 7, §5.

theologian, however much he specializes in exegesis, or church history, or what not, must keep the architectonic end of church government in view. Failing in this, his work has no overt theological significance, and he does not merit the name of theologian. Theological education must produce a general comprehension of all that appertains to the guidance of a particular church.[87]

But how is the *Kirchenfürst* to conceive his particular church and the interests involved in its government? He must go to the past, study the history of his church, and learn largely from that source what it is and what it needs. He cannot spin an adequate conception of his office from some abstract principles, or from his own private experience and the desire of his heart. Schleiermacher lays great emphasis upon historical study as providing the material with which reason must work if it is to be in effective touch with concrete reality. He shows a full appreciation of Bacon's famous dictum, so proverbially neglected by theologians: "the wit and mind of man, if it work upon matter . . . worketh according to the stuff and is limited thereby; but if it work upon itself, as the spider worketh its web, then it is endless, and brings forth indeed cobwebs of learning, admirable for the fineness of thread and of work, but of no substance or profit."[88] Moreover, Schleiermacher speaks of historical study as if it gave not only material for the mind to work upon, but also in part a direction in which to work. He seems to agree in a measure with Aristotle that things have a proper course of development, im-

[87] *Werke*, I, v. 1, p. 7, §§6-8.
[88] Francis Bacon, *The Advancement of Learning*.

plicit in them from their beginnings. Historical science can, therefore, reveal to the *Kirchenfürst* the lines along which the further progress of his church lies.[89]

In order to do this, however, historical study must be wedded to philosophy. For a purely empirical study of events will not suffice to distinguish the essential from the accidental, and not every event in the history of a church is to be regarded as essential. In fact, some are to be viewed as errors, and the *Kirchenfürst* must be trained to recognize them as such even in the germ, that is, in their very first beginnings.[90] In the Christian church it is the function of what Schleiermacher calls "philosophical theology," first to distinguish Christianity from other religions (apologetics), and secondly, to define the true Christianity as distinguished from its excrescences (polemics).[91] To accomplish this work of discrimination philosophical theology must bring to bear upon the facts of Christian history a wisdom gained from ethics, a general comprehension of reasonable being, and from the philosophy of religion, a critical survey of religion in its various forms.[92] The generalizations of speculative philosophy and the specific researches of history must supplement and validate each other in fixing the locus of a church.

The chief generalizations from his ethics and from

[89] *Werke*, I, v. 1, pp. 14-15, §§26-28; p. 34, §70. Schleiermacher divides the field of theological study into three parts: philosophical, historical, and practical theology, each of which supplements the others so as to form with them an organic whole.
[90] *Werke*, I, v. 1, pp. 12-13, §§21-24, p. 18, §§35-36.
[91] *Werke*, I, v. 1, pp. 18-30, §§35-62.
[92] *Werke*, I, v. 1, p. 18, §35, p. 13, §23.

his philosophy of religion, which Schleiermacher brings to bear upon Christian history in order to fix the locus of his own church, are briefly set forth in the introduction to his *Der christliche Glaube*. First and foremost is the proposition that "the essential basis of a church is piety, a state of feeling rather than of knowledge or of morals."[93] This, of course, is the central point in his theory of religion as given in the *Speeches on Religion*. But in *Der christliche Glaube* he adds a thesis as to the general character of piety, which helps to identify religious feeling more specifically. The feelings which accompany our thoughts and deeds are of two kinds, he says, those in which we feel ourselves to be passive, receptive, suffering affectation from without, and those in which we feel ourselves as active or expressive, as effecting changes in something beyond us. There are no feelings, he holds, in which we sense ourselves as purely and completely active without a trace of receptivity, but there are feelings in which we feel that even our own activity is received from something not ourselves. These feelings of absolute dependence (*schlechthinniges Abhangigkeitsgefühl*) are the religious feelings.[94] This emphasis upon dependence as the criterion of religious feeling is not absent from Schleiermacher's early writings. The pietistic consciousness of his boyhood was primarily one of repose in God. But in the *Speeches,* religious feeling is represented not only as a sense of dependence on the Universe, but also as an aspiration toward, as an openness to the Universe.[95] In placing greater emphasis on the feeling

[93] *Werke,* I, v. 3, p. 6.
[94] *Werke,* I, v. 3, p. 15.
[95] See above p. xlviiff.

of dependence in his later writings Schleiermacher brought his view of religion closer to traditional Christian theology.

This religious sense of absolute dependence, he regards as a natural element in human consciousness, not to be derived from or supplanted by any other. Hence the church, resting on such piety, is a natural group like the family, like the state, permanently rooted in human nature. It is not an association formed to serve a temporary need of certain human societies. A church is a communion of individuals having a similar sense of dependence upon the Universe.[96] Theologies and rituals express various aspects of the life of such communions, but the nucleus of a church is the piety that pervades it. The *Kirchenfürst*, therefore, must comprehend his church in the light of its piety, understanding its creed and practice by reference to that, and not *vice versa*. The essential, architectonic wisdom for an ecclesiastic is a knowledge of the religious sense peculiar to his church, for without the leaven of that knowledge all theological and liturgical learning remains heavy and inert.

But how is this animating principle of religion revealed to the soul? Is the inner light of theological wisdom a free gift of God, or is there some discipline by which religious insight can be perfected at its very center? Schleiermacher holds that a comparative study of religions, if carried on in a philosophic spirit, is very helpful.[97] For such study reveals, as it were, the dimensions of piety, its essential factors, and in so doing gives an approach, at least, by way of defini-

[96] *Werke*, I, v. 3, p. 32.
[97] *Werke*, I, v. 3, pp. 38-67. Cf. *Werke*, I, v. 1, pp. 17-18, §§32-33ff.

tions to the indefinable, religious emotions themselves. If we are to know a specific form of piety, we must know, first of all, the character of its emotional organization. This is its first dimension. The second is the view of the universe with which this emotional organization is fused. And the third is the historic context or tissue of events significantly related to the other two. From his own comparative researches Schleiermacher comes to the conclusion that the most important difference in emotional organization, from the religious point of view, is the difference between an esthetic and a teleological organization of the emotions. In esthetic piety the impulses toward a natural enjoyment of the immediate predominate over the impulses making for moral reform; in teleological piety the reverse is the case. Mohammedanism is mainly esthetic, Judaism and Christianity teleological. The latter are differentiated emotionally from each other in that the first expresses primarily a need for reconciliation, the second for redemption. These three great religions are thus very different in respect to their emotional character, but they all seem to Schleiermacher to be on the same metaphysical level, namely, that of monotheism. He believes there is a progress discernible in man's knowledge of the universe from a state wherein the idea of a universe or totality of things is entirely absent from human imagination to the state wherein men begin to conceive the whole of things vaguely as an interplay of powers, and finally to a conception of the universe as one great ordered system, the idea of modern science. Religious emotion combined with ideas of the first stage in metaphysical development gives rise to fetichism, in which piety is referred to some specific object rather than to the whole of things. Then come the various stages of polytheism, and finally monotheism. Judaism, Christianity, and Mohammedanism are all on the monotheistic level. Pantheism is treated as a variant of monotheism, arising in the endeavor to minimize anthropomorphism in the conception of the Deity. Thus, Schleiermacher, believing that the metaphysical development of humanity through the progress of science is toward a conception of an Infinite Whole, believes also that there is a progress in religion towards monotheism. But he develops no theory of progress in the religious emotions themselves. Likewise, he has no general theory as to the nature of that tissue of historical events which, according to him, is also part and parcel of every living religion, a third dimension, as it were, of piety. The only generalization which he ventures in this regard is the observation that first beginnings are extremely important in religion. Thus in Christianity everything is referred back to Christ, and the influence of the early Christians is persistent.[98]

On the basis of such theories and inquiries Schleiermacher defines Christianity as "a monotheistic religion, in which piety is teleological and focussed upon the redemption wrought by Christ."[99] Every *Kirchenfürst*, he holds, must pursue a similar quest for such guiding concepts and definitions, if he would wisely compass the practical end of church government. The quest is historical and philosophic: neither historical learning, nor philosophical speculation alone will suf-

[98] *Werke*, I, v. 3, pp. 38-67. Cf. this whole analysis of piety, which Schleiermacher called his "philosophy of religion," with the fifth of the *Speeches on Religion*. See above pp. li-liii.
[99] *Werke*, I, v. 3, p. 67.

fice, but each must supplement the other in order to yield the kind of theoretic insight which has significance for practice.[100]

In describing the historical equipment of a *Kirchenfürst*, Schleiermacher is fully as constructive as in his treatment of the philosophical aspects of ecclesiastical education, for he had both a craftsman's acquaintance with the tools of research and a well-considered ideal of historical study.[101] His whole habit of mind was appreciative of the past, and following the impulse of this appreciation he discovered, in a measure unusual for his time, the outlines of cultural history in Europe. He was convinced that a general survey of human history as a whole is indispensable to the *Kirchenfürst*, since the development of churches and religions can be understood only in connection with the development of all mankind.[102] But while advocating this broad perspective, he also laid great emphasis on the importance of exegesis, for his analysis of piety had caused him to believe that an accurate knowledge of a religion in its first beginnings is very helpful to an understanding of its essence.

Exegesis, therefore, being the study of a religion in its original forms and documents, is the most important single department of historical study for the *Kirchenfürst*. Schleiermacher makes the requirements in this field very stringent, and outlines them thoroughly. "Every specialist in exegesis must be able to construe the text of the canon critically, while every theologian, whether specializing in exegesis or

[100] *Werke*, I, v. 1, p. 15-16, §§29-31.
[101] *Werke*, I, v. 1, pp. 34-100, §§69-256. See also above p. 120 and note.
[102] *Werke*, I, v. 1, pp. 40, §§85-86, p. 66, §165.

no, must master the principles and methods of historic criticism, and must have a general knowledge of the most important critical sources and their relative worth."[103] The Christian church must develop an expert knowledge of ancient languages among its own theologians, since the canonical writings are not interesting enough from the purely linguistic point of view to secure adequate critical attention from lay scholars.[104] Such attention is a constant requirement of the church, for the work of critically interpreting the canon can never be regarded as completed. Exegesis is a permanent discipline, repeatedly furnished with fresh problems by new discoveries and by the growing intellectual sensibility of mankind.[105]

Though Schleiermacher's account of exegetical science in his *Brief Exposition of Theological Studies* is very full and illuminating, the general spirit and the philosophical presuppositions of his own exegetical work can be appreciated still better by examining his specific contributions to the field. For instance, an examination of his *Life of Jesus* shows that he treats the Gospels as historical narratives, inaccurate perhaps in certain respects, but valuable, nevertheless, as recording actual events of religious significance. This attitude assumes that the religious significance of the Gospels is lodged in the events they narrate rather than in the narration itself or in the spirit of the writer. If it were primarily in the latter, the historic validity of the Gospels might be a matter of secondary importance. But Schleiermacher does not treat it so; he takes the records, and tries to construct therefrom a narrative,

[103] *Werke*, I, v. 1, p. 53, §§123-124.
[104] *Werke*, I, v. 1, pp. 60-61, §147.
[105] *Werke*, I, v. 1, p. 60, §145, p. 46ff., §103.

160 SCHLEIERMACHER'S SOLILOQUIES

which he regards as both historically valid and religiously significant. For example, in his discussion of the Virgin Birth, he maintains not only that a Virgin Birth would have no religious value, but also that the Gospels do not declare it to have been a fact.[106] Similarly, in his treatment of the miracles of Jesus, he tries to show that the Gospels report as facts only such happenings as make the miracles religiously valuable.[107]

Schleiermacher conceived the divinity of Jesus to consist in his special relation to God, whereby he awakened in other men the Christian consciousness of redemption. Thus, in his treatment of the Gospel narrative he prefers the Johannine emphasis upon Jesus's message, and the significance of its eternal truth for the human soul.[108] But he also accepts as historically correct many of the incidents emphasized in the other Gospel accounts of Jesus's life. He believes, for example, that Jesus did effect remarkable cures, and he believes also in the resurrection. He insists, however, that these unique acts and powers of Jesus must be regarded as fully compatible with human nature when spiritually perfected by the influence of God.[109] Jesus, that is, was fully human, and at the same time so perfected. From these observations it follows that Schleiermacher was a supernaturalist, if it be supernaturalism to believe in the resurrection and in the cures of Jesus. But if supernaturalism means that

---

[106] *Werke*, I, v. 6, pp. 58-64. This *Life of Jesus* had considerable influence upon D. F. Strauss's better known work.

[107] *Werke*, I, v. 6, pp. 206ff.

[108] *Werke*, I, v. 6, pp. 225, 245, 273ff. Cf. this *Life of Jesus* with the *Speeches on Religion*, p. 246ff. And see pp. lii-liii. also Schleiermacher's *Weinachtsfeier*, a dialogue on the theme of Christ's significance.

[109] *Werke*, I, v. 6, pp. 214ff.

the world of God is not the natural world, but another world, then Schleiermacher was not a supernaturalist. For he believed that in truth there is but one order of things, the order of God.

That Schleiermacher was so much concerned with the interpretation of the Gospels may suggest a strong strain of traditionalism, if not of authoritarianism, in his thought. But he never abandoned his conception of religion as a free field for individuality, nor his idea of the church as a fluid association. He only emphasized more and more the intellectual responsibility of the individual, and especially of the *Kirchenfürst*, to conceive correctly the real relations between his religion and that of others. The moral of Schleiermacher's attention to the past was not conservatism, but individualism through spiritual finesse. Exegesis and church history are not intended to bind the individual, but to help him discover himself through the study of others. At least, this is where the emphasis falls. The *Kirchenfürst* is intellectually and spiritually obligated to recognize heresy as heresy and schism as schism; such recognition, however, does not imply that what is heretical or schismatic from the point of view of his own church is any less valuable to mankind than his orthodoxy, or any less religious.[110]

But what is heretical from the point of view of a given church? How is the *Kirchenfürst* to answer that question? He must put himself on the track of orthodoxy by taking his religious symbols from a source recognized by his church, and he must follow a certain rationale in their interpretation. This method will not lead him to conclusions which all orthodox

[110] *Werke,* I, v. 1, pp. 74-80, §§203-204.

members of his church accept fully and exactly, for even within orthodoxy there are individual differences, but it will keep him within the field of orthodoxy.[111] Schleiermacher is no innovator in his conception of the sources from which orthodox religious symbols are to be drawn, for he holds that a religious symbol must have the sanction of tradition or of general recognition within the church for which it is considered orthodox. Thus, in the case of the Evangelical Church all propositions which claim to be dogmas must call to witness either the Evangelical Confessions, or the New Testament, or a general recognition by the church of their dogmatic character.[112] But he is most original in his idea of the rationale by which authenticated religious symbols are to be interpreted. This, in fact, is the point at which his general theory of religion is in closest and most fruitful touch with his theology.

The first step in the interpretation of religious symbols is for the *Kirchenfürst* to discriminate between different kinds of symbols, Schleiermacher distinguishes between three main types: poetic, hortatory, and didactic (*dichterische, rednerische, und darstellend belehrende*). Didactic symbols which arise in the attempt to teach or instruct, are more stable in meaning than poetic or hortatory symbols, and hence a logic of their interpretation can be more definitely formulated.[113]

The cardinal principle in Schleiermacher's interpre-

[111] *Werke*, I, v. 1, pp. 76-77, §196.
[112] *Werke*, I, v. 3, p. 144.
[113] *Werke*, I, v. 3, pp. 99-107 ff. Schleiermacher was personally interested in poetic and hortatory symbolism as well as in dogmatics. It is scarcely necessary to remark this of so great a preacher. He also participated in editing a Hymnology and in many decisions of the Evangelical Church regarding ritual.

tation of didactic symbols or dogmas is to regard them in the light of the religious consciousness from which they spring. Consider, for example, the dogma that God created the world. It would be a mistake, says Schleiermacher, to interpret this doctrine as a scientific proposition about God and the world, to seek empirical verification of it, or to look for some first principles from which it can be logically deduced. Human experience and human reason will not suffice to establish such a proposition in the sense in which the religious man believes it. If that sense is to be preserved, the dogma must be viewed as a confession of faith, that is, as the expression of a certain consciousness in which the man feels the world to be dependent upon God.[114] The function of the dogma is to communicate that consciousness. Consider another example. In the Christian tradition theologians have wrestled much with the "problem of evil." Dogma says that God is omnipotent and all-good. Why then is there evil? Schleiermacher suggests that the difficulty arises from treating these dogmas as verifiable descriptions of fact, which must be rendered consistent with each other. But the *Kirchenfürst*, the wise man who knows religion well, will take them as a system of symbols appropriate to the expression of Christian religious feeling. The Christian has a double consciousness, a sense of the divine and a sense of that which is not divine. The latter, existing in him together with the former, gives him a conviction of his own imperfection. Yet he also has a faith that the consciousness of the divine can supplant the other consciousness, as in Christ, and that

[114] *Werke*, I, v. 3, pp. 182ff.

then he would be perfect, lacking nothing.[115] Such are the feelings which these Christian dogmas express. "The problem of evil" is not a problem to be solved by the theoretic reconciliation of propositions, but rather a religious problem, involving the triumph of one state of consciousness over another. A system of dogmas is not a logical system, but a system of things felt in the religious mind. The *Kirchenfürst* will not try, therefore, to deduce one dogma from another, but will trace each back to the original feeling which brought it forth, and which sustains, justifies and explains it.[116]

In accordance with this fundamental principle Schleiermacher tries to interpret the dogmas of Evangelical Christianity as a system of religious symbols expressing a consciousness of triumph over sin and evil through the redemption wrought by Christ. This is the main idea underlying his chief work on dogmatic theology, *Der christliche Glaube*, a work of beautiful lucidity in which both the strength and limitations of his thought stand clearly revealed. It was not his achievement to give the great religious concepts of sin and evil and redemption a deeper meaning. His essential accomplishment was to view these concepts as applying to a kind of experience that could be assimi-

[115] *Werke*, I, v. 4, pp. 6ff.

[116] This is the new principle in Schleiermacher's interpretation of dogma, but he compromises with tradition in many ways. In *Der christliche Glaube* he finds it necessary to present the dogmas of the Church in three different aspects: (1) as descriptions of God, (2) as descriptions of God's relations to the world, (3) as descriptions of human feeling in the presence of God. But he hastens to add that "it is an analysis of religious consciousness which must underlie all three of these presentations as the only scientific basis for the interpretation of dogma." See *Werke*, I, v. 3, pp. 160-164.

lated to other kinds of experience, in particular to modern science and morals. His true originality, like that of his contemporaries in German philosophy, was speculative, and the main trend of his speculation was to mediate between the various kinds of value to which he was sensitive. His work is characterized throughout by the attempt to do justice to divergent interests. He sought to combine the preservation of religious traditions with the fullest development of science and of individualized morality. No mind more perfectly illustrates the mediating character of thought in the early nineteenth century than does Schleiermacher's in the second half of his life. At the same time, his speculation culminates, as the speculation of a mind tinged with romantic idealism should culminate, in the conception of an infinite task with infinite opportunities of salvation. For the harmonious adjustment of different human interests is an infinite task, and where the interests involved are those of knowledge, personality, and communion with the universe, who can doubt that salvation is near at hand?

SELECTED BIBLIOGRAPHY

I. Schleiermacher's Works

German works marked with an asterisk (*) have been translated into English, in whole, or in part.

Sämmtliche Werke. Berlin, Reimer, 1835-'64. 31 volumes. Referred to in this text as *Werke*. Published in three parts, theological, homiletical, and philosophical, cited as I, II, and III respectively.

Schleiermachers Werke: Auswahl in vier Bänden. Leipzig, Meiner, 1910-'13. A convenient collection of major works. Volume II is especially important as offering the first critical edition of the manuscripts on ethics in the Berlin archives.

*Aus Schleiermacher's Leben, in Briefen. Berlin, Reimer, 1858-'63. 4 volumes. Referred to as *Briefe*. Volumes 1 and 2 were translated into English by F. Reivan, London, 1860. These are cited as *Letters*.

*Über die Religion. Critical editions by G. C. B. Pünjer, Braunschweig, 1879, and R. Otto, Göttingen, 1899, 4th ed., 1920. Referred to as *Reden*. Translated into English by John Oman, London, 1894, and cited as *On Religion*.

*Monologen. Critical edition by F. M. Schiele, Leipzig, Meiner, 1902. Contains an excellent bibliography on Schleiermacher's ethics, pp. xxxvi-xlviii. Referred to as *Schiele*. A French translaton of the *Monologen*, 3rd edition, by Louis Segond was published at Geneva and Paris, 1837, and 1864.

Grundlinien einer Kritik der bisherigen Sittenlehre. Critical edition by Herm. Mulert, Leipzig, Meiner, 1908.

Dialektik. Critical edition by J. Halpern, Berlin, 1903.

Schleiermachers Entwurfe zu einem System der Sittenlehre. Critical edition of the manuscripts on ethics in the Berlin archives, by Otto Braun. This is volume II of the *Auswahl*, mentioned above, Leipzig, Meiner, 1913.

*WEIHNACHTSFEIER. Critical edition by Herm. Mulert, Leipzig, Dürr, 1908. Translated into English by W. Hastie, 1890.
*KURZE DARSTELLUNG DES THEOLOGISCHEN STUDIUMS. Critical edition by Heinr. Scholz, Leipzig, 1910, published in Quellenschriften zur Geschichte des Protestantismus, Heft 10. Translated into English by William Farrer, Edinburgh, 1850.
*DER CHRISTLICHE GLAUBE, NACH DEN GRUNDSÄTZEN DER EVANGELISCHEN KIRCHE IM ZUSAMMENHANGE DARGESTELLT. Good editions are to be found in *Werke*, I., vols. 3 and 4, and in the Bibliothek theologischer Klassiker, Bd. 13-16, Gotha, 1889. Part I of a critical edition by Carl Stange appeared at Leipzig, 1910. *The Theology of Schleiermacher* by George Cross, Chicago, 1911, contains much of *Der christliche Glaube* in translation or paraphrase.

Significant early manuscripts and notes are published in part by Wilhelm Dilthey in an Appendix to his *Leben Schleiermachers*, Berlin, Reimer, 1870, cited as *Dilthey*, Appendix.

For further works and editions see the exhaustive bibliography in Ueberwegs, *Grundriss der Geschichte der Philosophie*, 11th edition, revised by K. Oesterreich, vol. IV, pp. 102-104.

II. COMMENTARIES

BAUER, JOH. *Schleiermacher als patriotischer Prediger*, Giessen, Töpelmann, 1908. Helpful for understanding Schleiermacher's relation to public life and practical affairs.
BENDER, WM. *Schleiermacher's Theologie*, Nördlingen, Beck, 1876.
CROSS, GEORGE. *The Theology of Schleiermacher*, Chicago, University Press, 1911. A condensed presentation of his chief theological work, "The Christian Faith."
DILTHEY, WILHELM. *Leben Schleiermachers*. Berlin, Reimer, 1870. An absolutely indispensable work for the study of Schleiermacher, and a very valuable description of the Berlin romantic group. Referred to as *Dilthey*. The Appendix, pp. 1-145, publishes manuscript material from diaries, etc., which throws much light upon Schleiermacher's philosophic development. The new edition by Hermann Mulert, Berlin and Leipzig, DeGruyter, 1922, omits this Appendix, but adds more than 250 pages based on Dilthey's notes for a second volume, treating of Schleiermacher's life from 1800 to 1807. I cite this new edition as N. E.
DILTHEY, WILHELM. *Schleiermacher*. A fine brief account in the Allgemeine deutsche Biographie, vol. 31, 1890. Republished in vol. IV of Dilthey's *Gesammelte Schriften*. Important for the second half of Schleiermacher's life.

GUNDOLF, FRIEDRICH. *Schleiermachers Romantik*. A very fine criticism of the romantic spirituality of the *Monologen*. Published in Deutsche Vierteljahrsschrift fur Literaturwissenschaft und Geistesgeschichte, Bd. II, Heft 3, 1924-'25.

HAYM, RUDOLF. *Die romantische Schule*. Berlin, 1870. 3rd edition revised by Oskar Walzel. A standard work of fine penetration.

HAYM, RUDOLF. *Gesammelte Aufsätze*. Contains an illuminating review of Dilthey's *Leben Schleiermachers*.

HUBER, EUGEN. *Die Entwickelung des Religionsbegriffs bei Schleiermacher*. Leipzig, 1901. Careful comparison of Schleiermacher's various treatments of this theme.

LOEW, W. *Das Grundproblem der Ethik Schleiermachers in seiner Beziehung zu Kant's Ethik*, Berlin, 1914. Illuminating as to the problems raised by Kant and their significance for his successors.

PASCENDI GREGIS. This famous encyclical of Pius X, condemning modernism (see *The programme of modernism*, Putman, N. Y., 1908) while not mentioning Schleiermacher, gives a very clear exposition of the general philosophy of religion which he helped to produce, and of the objections advanced by the Roman Catholic Church.

SELBIE, WILLIAM. *Schleiermacher, a Critical and Historical Study*. London, Chapman and Hall, 1913. Presents Schleiermacher as a theologian, but offers little with reference to his philosophy.

TROELTSCH, E., NATORP, P., and others. *Schleiermacher, der Philosoph des Glaubens*. Berlin-Schöneberg, 1910. A very fine group of studies, presenting different sides of Schleiermacher's activity, as churchman, educator, statesman, and philosopher, in the perspective of contemporary scholarship and conditions.

WEHRUNG, G. *Der geschichtsphilosophische Standpunkt Schleiermachers*. Strassburg, 1907. Good for the setting of Schleiermacher's thought in the history of philosophy.

WILLICH, EHRENFRIED VON. *Aus Schleiermacher's Hause*. Berlin, Reimer, 1909. Intimate pictures of Schleiermacher's family life by his step-son.

The sections on Schleiermacher in Hasting's *Encyclopedia of Religion and Ethics*, and in J. T. Merz, *A History of European Thought in the Nineteenth Century*, are perhaps the best brief accounts in English.

For further commentaries see the comprehensive list in Ueberwegs, *Grundriss der Geschichte der Philosophie*, 11th edition, revised by K. Oesterreich, vol. IV, pp. 783-785.

INDEX

Action, 28, 38, 42.
Activity, inner xlv, 16, 82-83, 101-103.
Albertini, xvi.
Ambiguity, 133.
Anthropomorphism, 157.
Antitheses, in thought and reality, 137 ff.; in human nature, 34 ff.; in ethics, 145 ff.
Apologetics, 153.
Aristotle, xiv, 117 & note, 134, 152-153.
Art, xliii, xlix, 23-24, 34-37, 35 note, 55, 64-68, 88.
Artist, nature of the, 34 ff., 55.
Atheism, xlviii.
Athenaeum, The, xxxviii, xl.
Authority, religious, 1, 161-162; political, lvi, 146-149.
Autonomy, 101-103.
Bacon, Francis, 152.
Barby, xvi-xvii.
Being, thought and, 135 ff.
Berlin, xxxv-xxxvii, lv-lvi, 76-78 & notes; University of, 131, 150.
Bible, 1, 158-162.
Bibliography, 167-169.
Briefe, Schleiermacher's, vx & note.
Brinkmann, xxxiv.
Canon, 158-159 ff.
Certainty, xx, 26-27, 29.
Charité, xxxv
Christ, xii, vx-xvi, vxii, lii ff., 83 & note, 157, 159-161.

Christianity, xii ff., li-liii, lvii, 150-151, 156-157,163-164.
Church, 1, 147, 149 ff., 151-152, 154-155; Evangelical, 162; R e f o r m e d, xxv, xxxv, lvi-lvii; universal, 1.
Civilization, xliii-xliv, 50 ff.
Classical scholarship, xix, xxi ff., liv.
Community spiritual, xliv, 17, 54-56, 109 note 11.
Conduct, 29, 65 ff. and note.
Conscience, xlii-xliii, 27-29, 27 note.
Contemplation, 13, 22, 37; in relation to action, 23-24, 28, 42. See also "Self".
Conversion, xviii, xlii, 28-29.
Creation, 24, 163.
C u l t u r e, xxviii, xxxvii-xxxviii, 50 ff., 61 ff., 77; in relation to religion, xlvii ff.; See also "Self".
Death, xlvii, 86-88, 89.
Dependence, sense of, xviii, 105 note 23, 120, 142 and note, 154-155.
Der Christliche Glaube, Schleiermacher's lvii-lviii, 149-165.
Destiny, xliv-xlv, 69-70 ff., 77-81, 86 ff.
De Wette, lvi.
Dialectic, 134-142, 135 note.
Dialektik, Schleiermacher's 135 note.

Dichotomies, see "Antitheses".
Dilthey, Wilhelm, xiv note, 116 & note, 116 ff.
Disillusionment, xxxiii-xxxiv, 13.
Divine life, 22-23.
Division of labor, 51 ff.
Dogma, 161-165.
Dohna, family of Count. xxxiv-xxxv, 74, 124.
Doubts, religious, xvii-xix; moral, xxxiv, 29-30 ff.
Dreifaltigkeitskirche, lv-lvi.
Drossen, xxxiii.
Duty, xxxi-xxxii, xlii-xliii, 30-31 ff., 132-133, 145-148.
Eberhard, E. A., xix-xx, xxv.
Economic order, 51-53, 146-149.
Education, 60 & note, 146-149 & note; religious, 150-159 ff.
Ellerian sect, xiv.
Emotion, 17-18, 154 ff.; religious, xlvii-liii, 105 note 23, 154 ff.
Empiricism, xix-xx, xli-xliv, xlvi ff., 10-16, 73.
Epistemology, see "Knowledge".
Equality, 52-54 ff.
Equanimity, xviii, 42, 75 & note, 88.
Ethics, xxxi-xxxii, xlviii, 5-6, 26-33, 53, 98-103, 116-119, 124-125, 127-129, 141; relation to religion. xlviii. 22 & note, 117, 141; systematic ethics, 132-134, 142-149.
Evil, xlv, 92-94, 144; problem of, 163-164.
Exegesis, lvii, 131, 158-159 ff.
Experience, lviii-lix, 138, 141-142; religious, xviii, xxxii, xlvi-li, 22 & note, 25 & note, 38 & note, 120-121, 127-128, 140-142, 147, 154 f. See also "Empiricism".
Family, l-li, 57-58, 78-80, 146-149, 151, 155.
Feeling, see "Emotion".
Fetichism, 156-157.
Fichte, xxxv-xxxviii, xl, xliii, lv, 23 & note, 27 & note, 30-31 & notes, 71 & note, 132, 136 & note.
Frederick the Great, xxv, xxxvi.
Freedom, xxiii, xlii, xliv-xlv, lvi, 16-21, 28-29, 31-32, 60 & note, 69-75 ff., 101-103, 119, 144-145 & notes.
French Revolution, xxii-xxiii, xxxiii, liv, 62 & note, 74-75.
Friendship, xvii, xxxiii, xxxvii, xliii-xliv, 37, 43-48, 56-57, 74, 84-88, 146 ff.
Future, the, 56, 61 ff.
God, xviii, xlii, xlviii, 12, 24-25, 69-70, 87, 117, 120, 137, 140-142, 163-164.
Goethe, xxiv, xxxv-xxxviii.
Good, xxxi-xxxii, 132-134, 145 ff.; *summum bonum*, xxxi-xxxii, 116-117, 145-146; calculus of goods, 13-14.
Greek culture, see "Hellenism".
Grunow, Eleonore, liv, 78-80, 79 note, 86 & note.
Halle, University of, xvii-xxi, xxv, xxvii, lv, 131, 151 note.
Harmony, see "Equanimity".
Heaven, 17, 25, 117.
Hedonism, xxxi, 15, 116-117.
Hegel, xxi, xxviii, lvii, 120, 128 & note, 139-140, 148.

INDEX

Hellenism, xvii, xix, xxi-xxii, 77; see also "Classical scholarship".
Hengstenberg, lvi.
Herder, xxix, 76 & note, 121.
Herz, Madame, xxxvii, xli, 86 & note.
Heteronomy, 133.
Higher world, 12, 23.
Hilmer, xvi.
History, xxi, xxxvii, lvi-lvii, 76-77, 120, 142-143, 152-153, 157, 160. See also "Schleiermacher".
Humanity, xxviii, xliii, 17, 22, 27-29, 50, 74-76 ff.; kinds of, xliii, 34 ff., 106-107.
Ideal, xxxiii, 31-32, 50 ff., 71, 101-103, 145-146.
Idealism, xxx-xxxi, 16-17, 56, 92-94, 105-106, 129-130, 135-136 & notes, 140 & note, 164-165.
Imagination, xlv, 14, 33, 81-84.
Immortality, xlii, 24-25, 87-88.
Individuality, xxxii, xliii, xlix, l-li, 20, 30-34, 38-41, 56-60, 75-76, 95, 106-107, 123, 124-129, 136, 146-148; development of, 28-34, 38-41, 78-79, 106-107; individual and universal, xxxii, 30-34, 127-128 & note, 138-141, 146-148.
Infinite, xlii, xlvii-xlix, 12, 22, 120-122.
Intellect, 24 & note, 135-136 ff.
Inwardness, xi, xliv-xlv, 9, 15-16, 18, 21, 26-27, 43, 59, 66-68, 69, 82-83, 100-103.
Jakobi, 121.
Jena, xxxvi.
Judaism, li, 156-157.

Kant, xix, xxiv-xxxii, xl, xliii, 20 note, 30-32, 62 note, 74-75 & note, 116-123, 125-126, 132,138, 140, 141 & note.
"Kirchenfürst", philosopher-priest, 149 ff.
Knowledge, 13-14, 76-77; theory of, xix-xxi, 134-143. See also "Science".
Kritik der Sittenlehre, liv-lv, 132-134, 167.
Kurze Darstellung, lv, 151 ff., 168.
Laissez-faire, lvi, 59 & note, 148-149.
Landsberg, xxxv.
Language, 64-68, 136 note 52.
Law, xxii, xxviii ff., 101-103; moral, xxxi-xxxii, xliii, 29-31, 116-119 ff., 143-145; natural, xiii, xxii, xxxii, 119 ff., 143-145; legalistic thinking, xxviii ff.
Leibniz, xxv-xxviii, 123.
Leisure, xxxvii, 36, 43.
Liberalism, xii-xiv, lvi, 54, 109-110, 148-150.
Life, 5, 15-16, 22-23, 26, 69-70, 90 ff., 98 ff.; fruit and blossom of, 98-103; divine, 12, 23.
Logic, xix-xxi, 134-140.
Love, xliii, 37-39, 45, 78-81, 127-128.
Manners, xlvii, 65-68, 65 note.
Marriage, xliv, liv, 57-58, 78-81.
Materialism, 16-17, 51-52, 90-92 ff.,; see also "world", and "economic order".
Mathematics xxi-xxii, xxvii-xxviii, 12 & note.
Mechanism, 11, 69-70.

Meditation, xli-xlii; see also "Contemplation".
Metaphysics, xxvi-xxvii ff., xxxii, xlvii-xlix, 16-18, 105, 120-123, 125-130, 134 ff., 156-157; see also "Reality", & "Dialectic".
Metternich, lvi, 148-149.
Miracles, 67, 159-161.
Modernism, xii-xiv, 1, liii, lix-lx, 150-151, 162-165.
Mohammedanism, li, 156-157.
Monologen, Schleiermacher's, xi, xxxix-xlvi, 1-111 text, 128-130, 167.
Monotheism, 156-157.
Morality, see "Ethics".
Moral law, see "Law".
Moravians, xii-xviii, 28 & note, 74 & note, 85 & note, 127 & note, 154.
Nationalism, xxv, lv-lvi, 58-59, 109-110, 148-149.
Naturalism, xvii, 160-161; see also "Law, natural".
Natural history, 142-143.
Natural law, see "Law".
Natural religion, xxxii, xlvii-xlviii.
Nature, xxxii, xlvii-xlviii, 10, 36; relation to reason, 138-139, 145-146; human nature, see "Humanity"; see also "Materialism".
Necessity, xxxii-xxxiii, xlii, 14-15, 17-21, 69-71 ff.
Nicolai, xxxvi.
Niesky, xv.
Novalis, xxxviii, 87 & note.
Okely, 85 & note.
Old age, xlvi, 49, 89-103.
Oman, John, xviii note 9, 167.
Organ, of the spirit, 17, 19-20, 138-139, 145-147; organ and symbol, 19-20, 145-147; see also "Symbol".

Orthodoxy, 161-162.
Outwardness, 11,15; see "Inwardness".
Pantheism, xxxii, xlviii-xlix, 156-157.
Pascendi gregis, 1, 169.
Pedagogy, see "Education".
Perfection, 48 & note, 87-88.
Philistinism, xxxvi-xxxviii, 50-53 ff., 61 ff.
Philology, xix, lvii, 131.
Philosophy, xxvi-xxvii, 120, 134-135 ff, 153. See also "Schleiermacher"..
Physics, 142-143.
Pietists, see "Moravians".
Plato, liv, 131-132, 133-134.
Politics, lvi-lvii, 148-149 & note.
Pius x, 1.
Polytheism, 156-157.
Practice, 33, 36; and theory, 24, 28, 42, 149. See also "Contemplation".
Preaching, xviii-xix, xxxviii-xxxix, lv-lvi, 130. See also "Schleiermacher".
Present age, see "Philistinism".
Priest, 1; and philosopher, 150 ff.
Progress, xliii-xlix, 50 ff., 61-62; in religion, 156-157.
Protestantism, xii ff., xlv ff., 162 ff,; see also "Church".
Prussia, lv-lvii, 148-149, xxxvi.
Puritanism, xii, xxi- xxii.
Rationalism, xiii, xv, xix-xx, xxii, xxv-xxx, xxxvi, xlvi-xlviii, 30 ff., 132, 136, 159-164.
Reality, xix-xx, xxxii, xliv, xlvii, 16-17, 22, 30, 82, 121-123, 129, 135-139 ff.
Reason, xxvi-xxx, 30; relation to nature, 138-139, 145-146.

Receptivity, xliii, xlix, 26 ff., 37-39, 75-78 ff.; 164-165; see also "Activity", and "Love".
Reconciliation, religious, 156.
Redemption, lii, 156-157.
Reformed C h u r c h, see "Church".
Relativism, 137-139.
Religion, xviii, xxxix, lviii-lix, 117, 127-128, 149 ff.; philosophy of, xlviii-liii, 130 ff.; see also "Education", "Emotion", "Ethics", "Experience", "Natural religion". "Theology", etc.
Religions, historic, li-lii, 155-157.
Renunciation, 89 ff.
Romanticism, xi, xiii-xiv, xxii-xxv, xxx-xxxi, xxxv-xxxviii ff., xxxv, liii-liv, lviii-lx, 12, 63-68, 91, 95-96, 100-103, 124-128, 164-165; in Germany, xxiii-xxv; the "romantc school", xxxvii-xxxviii.
Rousseau, xxvi-xxvii.
Salvation, xv-xvi, xviii, 22-25, 163-165.
Sämmtliche Werke, Schleiermacher's, 130, 167.
Santayana, George, 136 note 51.
Schelling, xxi, xxviii, 128, 138-139.
Schlegel, Friedrich, xxi, xxviii, xxxvii-xl, liv, 35 & note, 40 & note, 86 & note, 94 & note, 130-131, 132.
Schleiermacher, his family, xii-xvii; education of, xv-xxi; personal development of, xxxiii-xxxv, liv ff., 28-48, 70-88, 115, 123-132; public career of, lv-lviii, 130-131, 149-150; development of his philosophical system, xix-xxi, xxxi-xxxii, xxxviii-xli, lvi-lviii, 115-149; complete works of, xx note, 130, 167; early manuscripts, of, xxxi-xxxiii, 115-123; autobiographical sections of the *Soliloquies*, 28-48, 70-88. For the discussion of individual published works, see italicized German titles.

Schlobitten, xxxiv, 74 & note, 124.
Schools, see "Education".
Schopenhauer, 55 & note, 136 & note.
Science, xxiii, xlvii, xlix, 40 & note 38, 76, 127, 130 & note, 142-143; method & philosophy of, xix-xxi, 136 & note, 142-143, 143-147. See also "System".
Self, 5-6. 13-15, 19, 21-22, 23-25, 70-72; self-analysis, 13-15, 21-22, 26-28 ff.; self-consciousness, 27-34, 38 ff., 102-103; self-development & cultivation, 38 ff., 53-60, 67, 70-75 ff.; Ideal self, 5-6, 23-25, 70-72. See also "Spirit".
Senses, 92-94; see also "Outwardness".
Sensitiveness, 30-32 ff., 42 & note; see also "Receptivity".
Sin. 6 & note, 50 & note, 144, 163-164.
Sittenlehre, Schleiermacher's, 134. 142-149, 167.
Slavery, 14-15, 70-73; negro, 54.
Society, xliv, 54-60, 109. 146-149; spiritual, see "Community". See also "State".
Soliloquies, Schleiermacher's, see *"Monologen"*.

Speeches on Religion, Schleiermacher's, see *"Uber die Religion"*.
Spinoza, xxxii, 71 & note, 119-123, 133-134.
Spirit, xlii, xlviii-xlix, 21, 24-25, 53 ff., 90-94, 128, 138-140, 145-146; its relation to the world, 16-17, 82-83, 105-106. See also "Organ" and "Symbol".
State, xliv, lvi, 58-59, 146-149.
Stolpe, liv, 131-132.
Strassburg, xxxvi.
Strauss, David F., 4 & note, 160 & note.
Summum bonum, xxxi-xxxii, 116-117, 132-134, 145-148.
Supernaturalism, see "Naturalism".
Symbol, intellectual, 119-120 ff.; theological, 161-164; of the spirit, see "Organ".
System, idea of, xix-xxi; philosophic, 130-149; ethical, 132-134, 145-149.
Theology, xvii-xix, xxv, xxvii, xxxii, xlvii-l ff., lvii-lviii, 24-25, 69-70, 117, 127, 137, 140-141, 149-165.
Theory, and practice, see "Practice".
Thought, 23-25, 134-142. See also "Being".
Tieck, Ludwig, xxxviii.
Time, 10-11, 12-15, 22-23, 25, 61-62, 90-91 ff.
Totality, xx, xlix, 137, 140-141, 156.

Truth, 135-136. See also "Knowledge", "Certainty", & "Science".
Uber die Religion, Schleiermacher's *Reden*, xi, xxxviii-xxxix, xlvi-liii, 127-128, 167.
Unconditioned, 121-123.
Universal, and individual, see "Individuality".
Universe, xxxii, xlix, liii, 16-18, 127, 137, 140-141, 156, 160-161, 163.
Utilitarianism, xlviii.
Variety, of goods, xxii, xxxiii-xxv, liii, lviii-lx, 31-32, 56-57 ff., 145-146, 165.
Veit, Dorothea, liv.
Virgin birth, 160.
Virtue, 29, 132-133, 145-148.
Von Willich, E., 3 note, 169.
Weihnachtsfeier, Schleiermacher's, 131, 160 & note, 168.
Weimar, xxxvi.
Will, 19-20, 57-58, 71-72 ff., 117-119, 141 & note. See also "Practice".
Wolf, F. A., xix.
Woman, 60 note, 80 & note.
World, xlii, 26, 49-68, 98-103, 137, 163; as mirror of the spirit, 10, 16-17; regeneration of the world, 61-68. See also "Universe".
Youth, xlvi, 49, 74, 89-103; eternal, 94 & note.

Made in the USA
San Bernardino, CA
01 September 2014